Christmas 2005

For Julie —

Someone who exemplifies
what a good woman
should be!

Love,
Cindy

The Psalms of David

illuminated by

JAMES S. FREEMANTLE

WILLIAM MORROW   75 YEARS OF PUBLISHING
An Imprint of HarperCollins*Publishers*

This book was originally published in 1982 by William Morrow and Company, Inc., and reissued in 2004.

THE PSALMS OF DAVID. Copyright © 1982 by Stephen Freemantle. All rights reserved. Printed in Thailand. No part of this book may be used or reproduced in any manner whatsoever without written permission except in the case of brief quotations embodied in critical articles and reviews. For information address HarperCollins Publishers Inc., 10 East 53rd Street, New York, NY 10022.

HarperCollins books may be purchased for educational, business, or sales promotional use. For information please write: Special Markets Department, HarperCollins Publishers Inc., 10 East 53rd Street, New York, NY 10022.

Library of Congress Cataloging-in-Publication Number 82-81936
ISBN 0-688-01312-0

05   10 9 8 7

Foreword

My father lived in India all his life. His father served with the army there, and had originally come from Yorkshire. His mother was of Irish stock, and lived to a great age, about 108 I believe. James Swan Freemantle was born at Trichinopoly in southern India in 1859. He had an ordinary sort of education and never had any special art instruction, but he probably trained as an engineering draftsman.

His family moved up to Bihar in northern India when I was quite young, and he used to paint the scenes he could see from the windows of the family home. He too joined the army and traveled throughout the Middle East, storing memories of the landscape which he used later in his life in *The Psalms of David*.

I do not know much about his first marriage except

that he had two children. In 1906 James Freemantle married Clara, fifteen years his junior and, like him, the parent of two children from a previous marriage. My parents' marriage was extremely happy, and Father loved Clara devotedly until the end of his life. *The Psalms of David* was begun at about the time they married and worked on periodically during their thirty years together. James was not a religious man, but he poured all the skills he possessed into his rendering of the psalms. Because they are such beautiful love poetry he saw his illumination of them as a testament to his love for Mother.

After he left the army, Father worked in the jails department for some time. I think that this was in southern India, where I was born at Vellore in 1912. Then we moved to Samastipur, where we lived for two or three years. I remember my father seated at a desk by the window with his paints, specially ordered from Winsor and Newton, spread out before him. He only used those paints and India ink, often taking many hours to do just a couple of lines of his fine detailed lettering. Then he would go back and add a wealth of decoration. Sometimes he would do the lettering with a paintbrush, making the bodies of the letters first and then adding the tails painstakingly so that no join would show. Thus, half a page a night represented good progress. In about 1916 we moved to Gorakhpur near the Nepalese border, and soon Father took a job on the railways, for with five children to send to school, he needed the concessionary fares.

The Psalms of David is full of vivid illustrations from those years—scenes and wildlife which can be readily identified. The brilliantly colored blooms of India are here—the purple sweet pea, the book flower which closes at night, great big jacaranda trees and magnificent poinsettias, highly scented mimosa and many others. There are yellow Indian poppies in Psalm 25, coconut palms in Psalm 44 and lovely wild violets in Psalm 100. The flame of the forest was a wonderful sight and the laburnums had clusters of flowers three to four feet long. There were canna lilies everywhere, flowering all year round, and wonderful violets. There is an Indian lark on page 42, a bigger bird than the British one; the hoppie butterfly, shown on page 143, is very weak and never goes out in the sun. Father used to collect drummer butterflies like the one shown on page 315. His keen observation of these and other animals is shown in the many pages decorated with storks, kingfishers and pheasants, and many other examples of flora and fauna.

There are many illustrations of familiar sights round Gorakhpur. There was a large lake where my parents used to go walking and there were often spectacular sunsets and moonrises. This lake appears on pages 12 and 13. Page 103 shows a Brahmin temple with a post and flags. The flags flown at mealtimes warned passersby not to step inside the shadow of the pole or the Brahmin's food would be contaminated and spoiled. Page 20 shows Chinese lanterns such as were used at home and page 21 shows a nearby church.

The Golden Temple at Amritsar appears on page 113. Page 159 shows a scene from the journey up to school. The school was at Mussooree, up at 7,500 feet above sea level and thought to be healthier for us children than the heat of the plains. There are also remembered scenes from his travels in the army— harbors and villages in Turkey, and ships at sea, as well as marvelously detailed reproductions of Middle Eastern buildings and scenes copied from Victorian travel books, revealing his draftsman's training in the eye for detail.

Page 166 marks the end of my father's first period of work on the psalms, and he must have finished on January 4, 1918, the day inscribed on the highly decorated ornamental dedication: "To my beloved wife, Clara, from her loving husband, James S. Freemantle." He started work on the book again in the late 1920s, when he was living about fifty miles from Lucknow in a tiny place called Jarwal Road, which was very lonely. There was no activity except for two or three trains a day passing through and nothing to see except the great variety of flowers which grew all year round. So he continued with the psalms.

The first few pages were very hurried with little decoration or embellishment, but by about page 185 you can see that he was again taking joy in the book and his style starts to broaden. Although not as richly decorated as the first half of the book, there are still some very fine illustrations, such as the jacaranda on page 266, the scene on page 277, and the ornamentation on page 307. His fine distinctive script does not falter or give any signs of old age.

My father finished *The Psalms of David* when living with my sister in Lucknow. He died of pneumonia within a year of finishing this book, in 1934.

—STEPHEN FREEMANTLE
    December 1981

To—
My Beloved Wife,
Clara
From—
Her Loving Husband
James S. Freemantle.
4 · January 1918.

THE PSALMS OF DAVID.

PSALM 1

1. The happiness of the godly. 4. The un-happiness of the ungodly.

Blessed is the man that walketh not in the council of the ungodly, nor standeth in the way of sinners, nor sitteth in the seat of the scornful.

2. But his delight is in the law of the LORD; and in HIS law doth he meditate day and night.

3. And he shall be like a tree planted by the rivers of water, that bringeth forth his fruit in his season; his leaf also shall not wither; and whatsoever he doeth shall prosper.

4. The ungodly are not so: but are like the chaff which the wind driveth away.

5. Therefore the ungodly shall not stand in the judgment, nor sinners in the congregation of the righteous.

6. For the LORD knoweth the way of the righteous: but the way of the ungodly shall perish.

PSALM 11

1. The kingdom of Christ. 10 Kings are ex-

-horted to accept it.

Why do the heathen rage, and the people im-=agine a vain thing?

2. The kings of the earth set themselves, and the rulers take counsel together, against the LORD, and against his anointed, <u>saying</u>.

3. Let us break their bands asunder, and cast away their cords from us.

4. He that sitteth in the heavens shall laugh: the LORD shall have them in derision.

5. Then shall he speak to them in his wrath, and vex them in his sore displeasure.

6. Yet have I set my king upon my holy hill of Zion.

7. I will declare the decree: the LORD hath said unto me, Thou <u>art</u> my Son; this day have I begotten thee.

8. Ask of me, and I shall give <u>thee</u> the heathen for thine inheritance, and the uttermost parts of the earth <u>for</u> thy possession.

9. Thou shalt break them with a rod of iron; thou shalt dash them in pieces like a potter's vessel.

10. Be wise now therefore, O ye kings; be instructed, ye judges of the earth.

11. Serve the LORD with fear, and rejoice with trembling.

12. Kiss the Son, lest he be angry, and ye perish from the way, when his wrath is kindled but a little. Blessed <u>are</u>

all they that put their trust in him.

PSALM III

The security of God's protection.

A Psalm of David, when he fled from Absolom his son.

LORD, how are they increased that trouble me! many are they that rise up against me.

2. Many there be which say of my soul, There is no help for him in GOD. Selah.

3. But thou, O LORD, art a shield for me; my glory, and the lifter up of mine head.

4. I cried unto the LORD with my voice, and he heard me out of his holy hill. Selah.

5. I laid me down and slept; I awaked; for the LORD sustained me.

6. I will not be afraid of ten thousands of peo-ple, that have set themselves against me round about.

7. Arise, O LORD; save me, O my GOD: for thou hast smitten all mine enemies upon the cheek bone; thou hast broken the teeth of the ungodly.

8. Salvation belongeth unto the LORD; thy blessing is upon thy people. Selah.

PSALM IV.

1. David prayeth for audience. 2. He reproveth and exhorteth his enemies. 6. Mans happiness is in God's favor.

To the chief Musician on Neginoth, A Psalm of David.

Hear me when I call, O GOD of my righteousness: thou hast enlarged me when I
was in distress; have mercy upon me, and hear
my prayer.

2. O ye sons of men, how long will ye turn my glory
into shame? how long will ye love vanity, and seek
after leasing? Selah.

3. But know that the LORD hath set apart him that
is godly for himself: the LORD will hear when I call
unto him.

4. Stand in awe, and sin not: commune with your own
heart upon your bed, and be still. Selah.

5. Offer the sacrifices of righteousness, and put your
trust in the LORD.

6. There be many that say, Who will show us any
good? LORD, lift thou up the light of thy countenance
upon us.

7. Thou hast put gladness in my heart, more than
in the time that their corn and their wine increased.

8. I will both lay me down in peace, and sleep;
for thou, LORD, only makest me dwell in

safety.

PSALM V.

1. David prayeth, and professeth his study in prayer. 4. God favoreth not the wicked. 7. David, professing his faith, prayeth unto God to guide him, 10. to destroy his enemies, 11. and to preserve the Godly.

To the chief Musician upon Nehiloth, A Psalm of David.

Give ear to my words, O LORD, consider my meditation.

2. Hearken unto the voice of my cry, my King and my GOD: for unto thee will I pray.

3. My voice shalt thou hear in the morning, O LORD; in the morning will I direct my prayer unto thee, and will look up.

4. For thou art not a GOD that hath pleasure in wickedness: neither shall evil dwell with thee.

5. The foolish shall not stand in thy sight: thou hatest all workers of iniquity.

6. Thou shalt destroy them that speak leasing: the LORD will abhor the bloody and deceitful man.

7. But as for me, I will come into thy house in the multitude of thy mercy: and in thy fear will I worship

toward thy holy temple.

8. Lead me, O LORD, in thy righteousness because of mine enemies; make thy way straight before my face.

9. For there is no faithfulness in their mouth; their inward part is very wickedness; their throat is an open sepulchre; they flatter with their tongue.

10. Destroy thou them, O GOD; let them fall by their own counsels; cast them out in the multitude of their transgressions; for they have rebelled against thee.

11. But let all those that put their trust in thee rejoice: let them ever shout for joy, because thou defendest them: let them also that love thy name be joyful in thee.

12. For thou, LORD, wilt bless the righteous; with favor wilt thou compass him as with a shield.

PSALM VI.

1 David's complaint in his sickness. 8. By faith he triumpheth over his enemies.

To the chief Musician on Neginoth upon Sheminith, A Psalm of David.

O LORD, rebuke me not in thine anger, neither chasten me in thy hot displeasure.

2. Have mercy upon me, O LORD, for I am weak: O LORD, heal me; for my bones

are vexed.

3. My soul is also sore vexed: but thou, O LORD, how long?

4. Return, O LORD, deliver my soul: oh save me for thy mercies' sake.

5. For in death _there_ _is_ no remembrance of thee: in the grave who shall give thee thanks?

6. I am weary with my groaning; all the night make I my bed to swim; I water my couch with my tears.

7. Mine eye is consumed because of grief; it waxeth old because of all mine enemies.

8. Depart from me, all ye workers of iniquity; for the LORD hath heard the voice of my weeping.

9. The LORD hath heard my supplication; the will receive my prayer.

10. et all mine enemies be ashamed and sore vexed: let them return and be ashamed suddenly.

PSALM VII.

1. David prayeth against the malice of his enemies, professing his innocency. 10. By faith he seeth his defence, and the destruction of his enemies.

Shiggaion of David which he sang unto the LORD, concerning the words of Cush the Benjamite.

O LORD my GOD, in thee do I put my
trust: save me from all them that persecute me, and
deliver me:

2. Lest he tear my soul like a lion, rending it in pieces,
while there is none to deliver.

3. O LORD my GOD, if I have done this; if there
be iniquity in my hands;

4. If I have rewarded evil unto him that was at peace
with me; (yea, I have delivered him that without cause
is mine enemy :)

5. Let the enemy persecute my soul, and take it; yea,
let him tread down my life upon the earth, and lay mine
honour in the dust. Selah.

6. Arise, O LORD, in thine anger, lift up thy-
-self because of the rage of mine enemies: and awake
for me to the judgement that thou hast commanded.

7. So shall the congregation of the people compass thee about:
for their sakes therefore return thou on high.

8. The LORD shall judge the people: judge me, O
LORD according to my righteousness, and according to
mine integrity that is in me.

9. Oh let the wickedness of the wicked come to an end; but
establish the just: for the righteous GOD trieth the hearts
and reins.

10. My defence is of **GOD**, which saveth the upright in heart.

11. **GOD** judgeth the righteous, and **GOD** is angry with the wicked every day.

12. If he turn not, he will whet his sword; he hath bent his bow, and made it ready.

13. He hath also prepared for him the instruments of death; he ordaineth his arrows against the persecutors.

14. Behold, he travaileth with iniquity, and hath conceived mis=chief, and brought forth falsehood.

15. He made a pit, and digged it, and is fallen into the ditch which he made.

16. His mischief shall return upon his own head, and his violent dealing shall come down upon his own pate.

17. I will praise the **LORD** according to his righ=teousness: and will sing praise to the name of the **LORD** most high.

PSALM VIII

GOD'S glory is magnified by his works, and by his love to man.

To the Chief Musician upon Gittith. A Psalm of David.

O LORD OUR LORD, how excellent

is thy name in all the earth! who hast set thy glory above the heavens.

2. **O**ut of the mouth of babes and sucklings hast thou ordained strength because of thine enemies, that thou mightest still the enemy and the avenger.

3. **W**hen I consider thy heavens, the work of thy fingers, the moon and the stars which thou hast ordained;

4. **W**hat is man, that thou art mindful of him? and the son of man, that thou visitest him?

5. **F**or thou hast made him a little lower than the angels, and hast crowned him with glory and honour.

6. **T**hou madest him to have dominion over the works of thy hands; thou hast put all things under his feet:

7. **A**ll sheep and oxen, yea, and the beasts of the field;

8. **T**he fowl of the air, and the fish of the sea, and whatsoever passeth through the paths of the seas.

9. **O LORD** our **LORD,** how excellent is thy name in all the earth!

PSALM IX.

1. David praiseth GOD for executing of judgement. 11. He inciteth others to praise Him. He prayeth that he may have cause to praise Him.

To the chief Musician upon Muth-lab-ben, A PSALM of David.

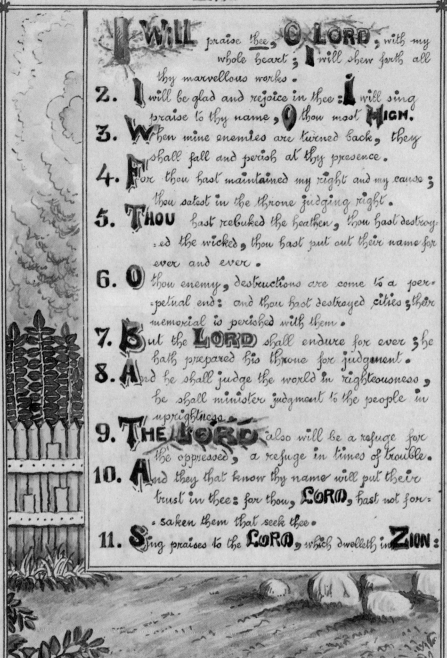

I will praise thee, **O Lord**, with my whole heart; I will shew forth all thy marvellous works.

2. I will be glad and rejoice in thee: I will sing praise to thy name, O thou most **High**.

3. When mine enemies are turned back, they shall fall and perish at thy presence.

4. For thou hast maintained my right and my cause; thou satest in the throne judging right.

5. **Thou** hast rebuked the heathen, thou hast destroy-ed the wicked, thou hast put out their name for ever and ever.

6. O thou enemy, destructions are come to a per-petual end: and thou hast destroyed cities; their memorial is perished with them.

7. But the **Lord** shall endure for ever; he hath prepared his throne for judgment.

8. And he shall judge the world in righteousness, he shall minister judgment to the people in uprightness.

9. **The Lord** also will be a refuge for the oppressed, a refuge in times of trouble.

10. And they that know thy name will put their trust in thee: for thou, **Lord**, hast not for-saken them that seek thee.

11. Sing praises to the **Lord**, which dwelleth in **Zion**:

declare among the people his doings.

12. When he maketh inquisition for blood, he remembereth them: he forgetteth not the cry of the humble.

13. Have mercy upon me, O LORD; consider my trouble which I suffer of them that hate me, thou that liftest me up from the gates of death:

14. That I may shew forth all thy praise in the gates of the daughter of ZION: I will rejoice in thy salvation.

15. The heathen are sunk down in the pit that they made: in the net which they hid is their own foot taken.

16. The LORD is known by the judgment which he executeth: the wicked is snared in the work of his own hands. Higgaion. Selah.

17. The wicked shall be turned into hell, and all the nations that forget GOD.

18. For the needy shall not alway be forgotten: the expectation of the poor shall not perish for ever.

19. Arise, O LORD; let not man prevail: let the heathen be judged in thy sight.

20. Put them in fear, O LORD: that the nations may know themselves to be but men. Selah.

PSALM X.

1. David complaineth to GOD of the outrage of the

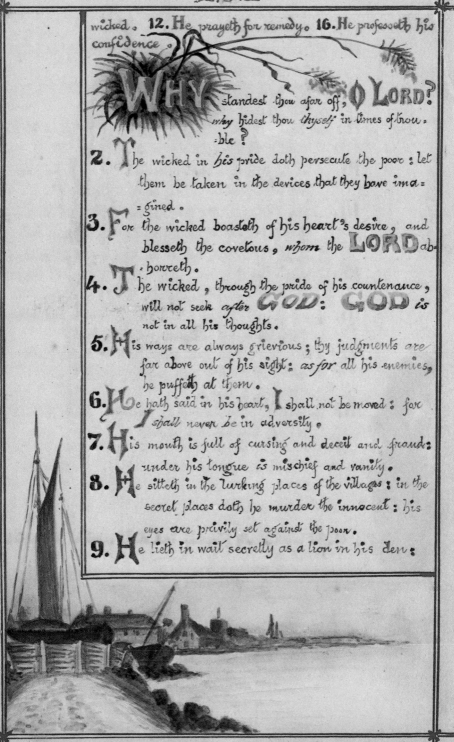

wicked. **12.** He prayeth for remedy. **16.** He professeth his confidence.

WHY standest thou afar off, O LORD? why hidest thou *thyself* in times of trouble?

2. The wicked in *his* pride doth persecute the poor : let them be taken in the devices that they have imagined.

3. For the wicked boasteth of his heart's desire, and blesseth the covetous, *whom* the LORD abhorreth.

4. The wicked, through the pride of his countenance, will not seek *after* GOD: GOD is not in all his thoughts.

5. His ways are always grievous; thy judgments are far above out of his sight: as for all his enemies, he puffeth at them.

6. He hath said in his heart, I shall not be moved : for I shall never be in adversity.

7. His mouth is full of cursing and deceit and fraud: under his tongue is mischief and vanity.

8. He sitteth in the lurking places of the villages : in the secret places doth he murder the innocent : his eyes are privily set against the poor.

9. He lieth in wait secretly as a lion in his den:

he lieth in wait to catch the poor : he doth catch the poor,
when he draweth him into his net.

10. He croucheth, and humbleth himself, that the poor may
fall by his strong ones.

11. He hath said in his heart, **GOD** hath forgotten : he
hideth his face ; he will never see it.

12. Arise **O LORD ; O GOD**, lift up thine
hand : forget not the humble.

13. Wherefore doth the wicked contemn **GOD?** he hath
said in his heart, Thou wilt not require it.

14. Thou hast seen it ; for thou beholdest mischief and
spite, to requite it with thy hand : the poor committeth
himself unto thee ; thou art the helper of the fatherless.

15. Break thou the arm of the wicked and the evil man :
seek out his wickedness till thou find none.

16. The **LORD** is **KING** for ever and ever :
the heathen are perished out of his land.

17. **LORD**, thou hast heard the desire of the humble :
thou wilt prepare their heart, thou wilt cause
thine ear to hear :

18. To judge the fatherless and the oppressed, that the man of
the earth may no more oppress.

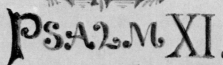

PSALM XI.

1. David encourageth himself in **GOD** against his enemies.

4. The providence and justice of GOD.
To the chief Musician, A Psalm of David.

IN THE LORD put I my trust: how say ye to my SOUL, Flee as a bird to your mountain?

2. For, lo, the wicked bend *their* bow, they make ready their arrow upon their string, that they may privily shoot at the upright in heart.

3. If the foundations be destroyed, what can the righteous do?

4. The LORD is in His Holy Temple, the LORD'S THRONE is in HEAVEN: His eyes behold, His eyelids try, the children of men.

5. The LORD trieth the righteous: but the wicked and him that loveth violence his soul hateth.

6. Upon the wicked He shall rain snares, fire and brimstone, and an horrible tempest: this shall be the portion of their cup.

7. For the righteous LORD loveth righteousness; His

countenance doth behold the upright.

PSALM XII.

1. David destitute of human comfort craveth help of GOD. 3. He comforteth himself with GOD'S judgements on the wicked, and confidence in GOD'S tried promises.

To the chief Musician upon Sheminith. A Psalm of David.

HELP, LORD; for the godly man ceaseth; for the faithful fail from among the children of men.

2. They speak vanity every one with his neighbour: with flattering lips and with a double heart do they speak.

3. The LORD shall cut off all flattering lips, and the tongue that speaketh proud things:

4. Who have said, With our tongue will we prevail; our lips are our own: who is lord over us?

5. For the oppression of the poor, for the sighing of the needy, now will I arise, saith the LORD; I will set him in safety from him that puffeth at him.

6. THE WORDS OF THE LORD ARE PURE WORDS: AS SILVER TRIED IN A FURNACE OF EARTH PURIFIED SEVEN TIMES.

7. Thou shalt keep them, O LORD, thou shalt preserve them from this generation for ever.

8. The wicked walk on every side, when the vilest men are exalted.

PSALM XIII.

1. David complaineth of delay in help. 3. He prayeth for preventing grace. 5. He boasteth of divine mercy.

To the chief Musician, A Psalm of David.

How long wilt thou forget me, O LORD? for ever? how long wilt thou hide thy face from me?

2. How long shall I take council in my soul, having sorrow in my heart daily? how long shall mine enemy be exalted over me?

3. Consider and hear me, O LORD my GOD: lighten mine eyes, lest I sleep the sleep of death;

4. Lest mine enemies say, I have prevailed against him; and those that trouble me rejoice when I am moved.

5. But I have trusted in THY mercy; my heart shall rejoice in THY SALVATION.

6. I will sing unto the LORD, because HE hath dealt BOUNTIFULLY WITH ME.

PSALM XIV

1. David describeth the corruption of a natural man. 4. He con=
=vinceth the wicked by the light of their conscience. 7. He glorieth in
the salvation of GOD.

To the chief Musician, A Psalm of David.

THE fool hath said in his heart, There is no
GOD. They are corrupt, they have done
abominable works, there is none that doeth good.

2. The LORD looked down from HEAVEN upon the
children of men, to see if there were any that did under=
=stand, and seek after GOD.

3. They are all gone aside, they are all together become filthy; there is none
that doeth good, no, not one.

4. Have all the workers of iniquity no knowledge? who eat up my people
as they eat bread, and call not upon the LORD.

5. There were they in great fear: for GOD is in the generation of the
righteous.

6. Ye have shamed the counsel of the poor, because the LORD is his
refuge.

7. Oh that the salvation of ISRAEL were come out of
ZION! when the LORD bringeth back the
captivity of HIS people, JACOB shall
rejoice, and ISRAEL shall be glad.

PSALM XV.

David describeth a citizen of Zion. A Psalm of David.

LORD who shall abide in THY taber=
=nacle ? Who shall dwell in
THY HOLY HILL?

2. HE that walketh uprightly, and worketh righteousness, and
speaketh the truth in his heart.

3. HE that backbiteth not with his tongue, nor doeth evil to his neigh=
=bour, nor taketh up a reproach against his neighbour.

4. IN whose eyes a vile person is contemned ; but he honoureth
them that fear the LORD. HE that swear=
=eth to his own hurt, and changeth not.

5. HE that putteth not out his money to usury, nor taketh
reward against the innocent. He that doeth
these things shall never be moved.

IN HELL; NEITHER WILT
THOU SUFFER THINE
+ HOLY + ONE +
TO SEE CORRUPTION.
11. THOU wilt show me the
path of life: IN THY
PRESENCE IS ✠
FULNESS OF JOY;
at thy right hand *there are* pleasures
for evermore.

PSALM XVII

1. David in confidence of his integrity, craveth de=
=fence of GOD against his enemies. 10.
He sheweth their pride, craft, and eager=
=ness. 13. He prayeth against them in
confidence of his hope.
A Prayer of David.

HEAR
the right
O LORD,
attend unto my
cry, give ear
unto my prayer,

that doeth not out of feigned lips.

2. **LET** my sentence come forth from thy presence; let thine eyes behold the things that are equal.

3. **THOU** hast proved mine heart; thou hast visited me in the night; thou hast tried me, *and* shalt find nothing; I am purposed *that* my mouth shalt not transgress.

4. **CONCERNING** the works of men, by the word of thy lips I have kept *me from* the paths of the destroyer.

5. **HOLD** up my goings in thy paths, *that* my footsteps slip not.

6. **I** have called upon thee, for thou wilt hear me, **O GOD:** incline thine ear unto me, *and hear* my speech.

7. **SHOW** thy marvellous lovingkindness, **O THOU** that savest by thy right hand them which put their trust *in thee* from those that rise up *against them.*

8. **Keep me as the apple of the eye, hide me under the Shadow of Thy wings.**

9. **FROM** the wicked that oppress, *from* my deadly enemies, *who* compass me about.

10. **THEY** are enclosed in their own fat: with their mouth they speak proudly.

11. **THEY** have now compassed us in our steps: they have set their eyes bowing down to the earth;

12. **LIKE** as a lion *that* is greedy of his prey, and as it were a young lion lurking in secret places.

13. **ARISE, O LORD,** disappoint him, cast him down: deliver my soul from the wicked, *which is* thy sword:

14. **FROM** men which are thy hand, **O LORD,** from men of the world, *which have* their portion in *this* life, and whose belly thou fillest with thy hid *treasure:* they are full of children, and leave the rest of their *substance* to their babes.

15. **AS** for me, I will behold thy face in righteousness: I shall be satisfied, when I awake, with thy likeness.

Psalm XVIII.

David praiseth GOD for his manifold and marvellous blessings. To the chief Musician, A Psalm of David, the servant of the LORD, who spake unto the LORD the words of this song in the day that the LORD delivered him from the hand of all his enemies, and from the hand of SAUL: And he said, _____

I WILL love thee, O LORD, my strength.

2. The LORD is my rock, and my fortress, and my deliverer; my GOD, my strength, in whom I will trust; my buckler, and the horn of my salvation, and my high tower.

3. **I** WILL CALL UPON THE **LORD**, WHO IS WORTHY TO BE PRAISED : SO SHALL I BE SAVED FROM MINE ENEMIES.

4. **The** sorrows of death compassed me, and the floods of ungod-ly men made me afraid.

5. **The** sorrows of hell compassed me about: the snares of death prevented me.

6. **In** my distress I called upon the **LORD**, and cried unto my **GOD** ; he heard my voice out of his temple, and my cry came before him, even into his ears.

7. **Then** the earth shook and trembled ; the foundations also of the hills moved and were shaken, because he was wroth.

8. **There** went up a smoke out of his nostrils, and fire out of his mouth devoured: coals were kindled by it.

9. **He** bowed the heavens also, and came down: and darkness was under his feet.

10. **And** he rode upon a cherub, and did fly : yea, he did fly upon the wings of the wind.

11. **He** made darkness his secret place ; his pavilion round about him were dark waters and thick clouds of the skies.

12. **At** the brightness that was before him his thick clouds pass-ed, hail stones and coals of fire.

13. **The LORD** also thundered in the heavens, and the **HIGHEST** gave his voice ; hail stones and coals of fire.

14. **Yea**, he sent out his arrows, and scattered them ; and he shot out lightnings, and discomfited them.

15. **Then** the channels of waters were seen, and the foundations of the world were discovered at thy rebuke **O LORD**, at the blast of the breath of thy nostrils.

16. **He** sent from above, **HE** took me, **HE** drew me out of many waters.

17. **He** delivered me from my strong enemy, and from them which hated me: for they were too strong for me.

18. **They** prevented me in the day of my calamity: but the **LORD** was my stay.

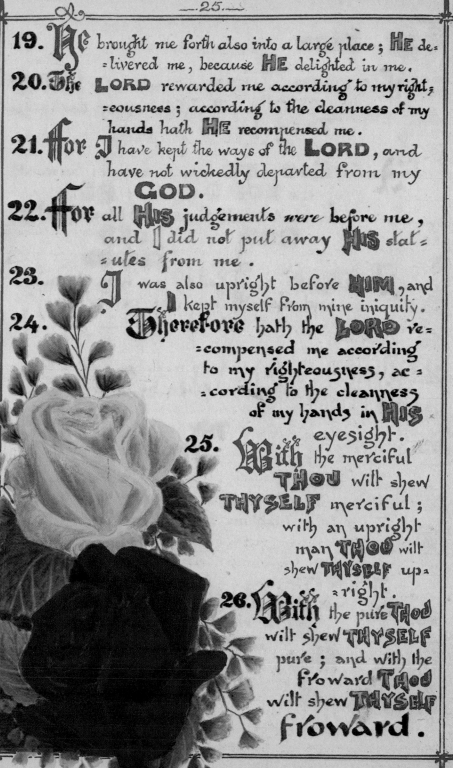

19. He brought me forth also into a large place; HE de=
=livered me, because HE delighted in me.

20. The LORD rewarded me according to my right=
=eousnees; according to the cleanness of my
hands hath HE recompensed me.

21. For I have kept the ways of the LORD, and
have not wickedly departed from my
GOD.

22. For all HIS judgements were before me,
and I did not put away HIS stat=
=utes from me.

23. I was also upright before HIM, and
I kept myself from mine iniquity.

24. Therefore hath the LORD re=
=compensed me according
to my righteousness, ac=
=cording to the cleanness
of my hands in HIS
eyesight.

25. With the merciful
THOU wilt shew
THYSELF merciful;
with an upright
man THOU wilt
shew THYSELF up=
=right.

26. With the pure THOU
wilt shew THYSELF
pure; and with the
froward THOU
wilt shew THYSELF
froward.

27. For **THOU** wilt save the afflicted people; but wilt bring down high looks.

28. For **THOU** wilt light my candle: the **LORD** my **GOD** will enlighten my darkness.

29. For by **THEE** I have run through a troop; and by my **GOD** have I leaped over a wall.

30. As for **GOD**, **HIS** way is perfect: the word of the **LORD** is tried: **HE** is a buckler to all those that trust in **HIM**.

31. For who is **GOD** save the **LORD**? or who is a rock save our **GOD**?

32. It is **GOD** that girdeth me with strength, and maketh my way perfect.

33. He maketh my feet like hinds' feet, and setteth me upon my high places

34. He teacheth my hands to war, so that a bow of steel is broken by mine arms.

35. Thou hast also given me the shield of **THY** sal:vation: and **THY** right hand hath holden me up, and **THY** gentleness hath made me great.

36. Thou hast enlarged my steps under me, that my feet did not slip.

37. I have pursued mine enemies, and overtaken them: neither did I turn again till they were consumed.

38. I have wounded them that they were not able to rise: they are fallen un::der my feet.

39. For **THOU** hast girded me with strength unto the battle: **THOU** hast sub::dued under me those that rose up against me.

47. It is GOD that avengeth me, and subdueth the people under me.

48. He delivereth me from mine enemies : yea, THOU liftest me up above those that rise up against me : THOU hast delivered me from the violent man.

49. Therefore will I give thanks un=to THEE, O LORD, among the heathen, and sing praises unto THY name.

50. Great deliverance giveth HE to HIS king; and shew=eth mercy to HIS anointed, to David, and to his seed for evermore.

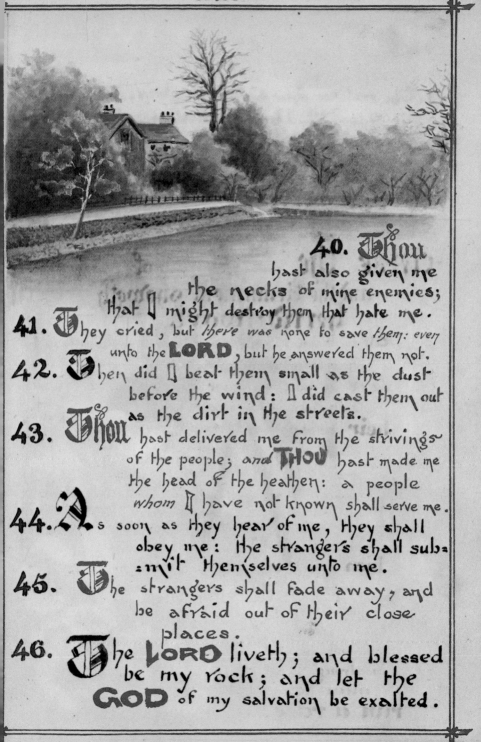

40. Thou hast also given me the necks of mine enemies; that I might destroy them that hate me.

41. They cried, but there was none to save them: even unto the LORD, but he answered them not.

42. Then did I beat them small as the dust before the wind: I did cast them out as the dirt in the streets.

43. Thou hast delivered me from the strivings of the people; and THOU hast made me the head of the heathen: a people whom I have not known shall serve me.

44. As soon as they hear of me, they shall obey me: the strangers shall submit themselves unto me.

45. The strangers shall fade away, and be afraid out of their close places.

46. The LORD liveth; and blessed be my rock; and let the GOD of my salvation be exalted.

PSALM XIX.

1. The creatures shew GOD'S glory. 7. The word his grace. 12. David prayeth for grace.
To the chief Musician, A Psalm of David.

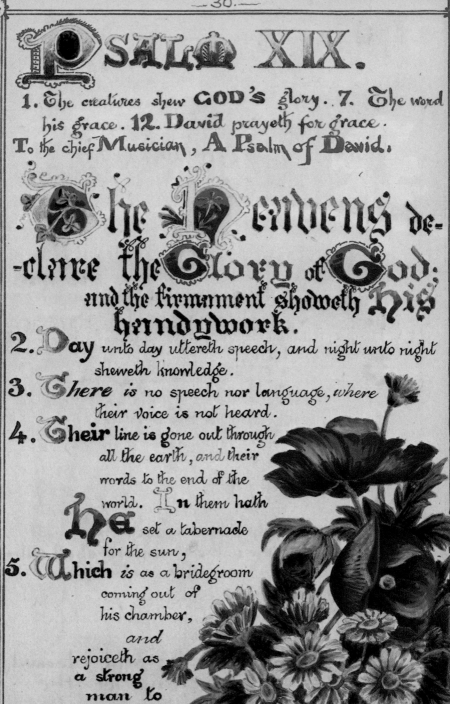

The Heavens declare the Glory of God: and the firmament showeth his handywork.

2. Day unto day uttereth speech, and night unto night sheweth knowledge.

3. There is no speech nor language, where their voice is not heard.

4. Their line is gone out through all the earth, and their words to the end of the world. In them hath he set a tabernacle for the sun,

5. Which is as a bridegroom coming out of his chamber, and rejoiceth as a strong man to run a race.

6. His going forth is from the end of the heaven, and His circuit unto the ends of it: and there is nothing hid from the heat thereof.

7. The LAW of the LORD is PERFECT, CONVERTING THE SOUL: THE TESTIMONY OF THE LORD IS SURE MAKING WISE the SIMPLE.

8. THE STATUTES OF THE LORD ARE RIGHT Rejoicing THE Heart: THE COMMANDMENT OF THE LORD IS PURE ENLIGHTENING THE EYES.

9. The fear of the LORD is clean, enduring for ever: the judgements of the LORD are true and righteous altogether.

10. More to be desired are they than gold, yea, than much fine gold: sweeter also than honey and the honeycomb.

11. Moreover by them is **THY** servant warned: *and* in keeping of them *there* is great reward.

12. Who can understand *his* errors? **CLEANSE THOU ME FROM SECRET FAULTS.**

13. Keep back thy servant also from presumptuous *sins;* let them not have dominion over me: then shall I be upright, and I shall be innocent from the great transgression.

14. Let the words of my mouth, and the meditation of my heart, be acceptable in **THY** sight, **O LORD**, my **STRENGTH**, and my **REDEEMER.**

PSALM XX.

1 The Church blesseth the king in his exploits. 7. Her confidence in **GOD'S** succour.

To the chief Musician. A Psalm of David.

THE LORD HEAR THEE IN THE DAY OF TROUBLE;

THE NAME OF THE GOD OF JACOB DEFEND THEE;

2. Send thee help from the **Sanctuary**, and strengthen thee out of **ZION**;

3. Remember all thy offerings, and accept thy burnt sacrifice; Selah.

4. Grant thee according to thine own heart, and fulfil all thy counsel.

5. WE WILL REJOICE IN THY SALVATION, AND IN THE NAME OF OUR GOD WE WILL SET UP *OUR* BANNERS: THE LORD fulfil all thy petitions.

6. Now know I that the LORD saveth HIS anointed; HE will hear him from HIS Holy Heaven with the saving strength of HIS right hand.

7. Some trust in chariots, and some in horses: but WE WILL REMEMBER THE NAME OF THE LORD OUR GOD.

8. They are brought down and fallen: but we are risen, and stand upright.

9. Save, LORD: let the KING hear us when we call.

PSALM XXI.

1 A Thanksgiving for victory. 7. Confidence of further success.

To the chief Musician, A Psalm of David.

THE KING

shall joy in THY strength, O LORD;

AND IN **THY SALVATION** HOW GREATLY SHALL HE REJOICE !

2. **THOU** hast given him his heart's desire, and hast not withholden the request of his lips. **Selah**.

3. For **THOU** preventest him with the blessings of goodness : **THOU** settest a 🕊 of pure gold on his head.

4. He asked life of **THEE**, and **THOU** gavest it him, even length of days for ever and ever.

5. His glory is great in **THY SALVATION** : honour and majesty hast **THOU** laid upon him.

6. For **THOU** hast made him most blessed for ever : **THOU** hast made him exceeding glad with **THY COUNTENANCE**.

7. For the king trusteth in the **LORD**, and through the **MERCY** of the **MOST HIGH** he shall not be moved.

8. **THINE HAND** shall find out all **THINE** enemies : **THY** right **HAND** shall find out those that hate **THEE**.

9. **Thou** shalt make them as a fiery oven in the time of **THINE** anger : the **LORD** shall swallow them up in **HIS** wrath, and the fire shall devour them.

10. Their fruit shalt **THOU** destroy from the earth, and their seed from among the children of men.

11. For they intended evil against **THEE** : they imagined a mischievous device, which they are not able to perform.

12. Therefore shalt **THOU** make them turn their back, when thou shalt make ready thine arrows upon **THY** strings against the face of them.

13. Be **THOU** exalted, **LORD**, in **THINE** own strength : so will we sing and praise **THY** power.

PSALM XXII.

1 David complaineth in great discouragement. 9. He prayeth in great distress. 23. He praiseth GOD.

To the chief Musician upon Aijeleth Sharar. A Psalm of David.

MY GOD, my GOD, why hast **Thou** forsaken me? why art **Thou** so far from helping me, and from the words of my roaring.

2. **O** my **GOD**, **I** cry in the daytime, but **Thou** hearest not; and in the night season, and am not silent.

3. But **THOU** art holy, **O THOU** that inhabitest the praises of **ISRAEL.**

4. **O**ur fathers trusted in **THEE**: they trusted, and **THOU** didst deliver them.

5. **T**hey cried unto **THEE**, and were delivered: they trusted in **THEE**, and were not confounded.

6. **B**ut **I** am a worm, and no man; a reproach of men, and despised of the people.

7. **A**ll they that see me laugh me to scorn: they shoot out the lip, they shake the head, saying,

8. He trusted on the **LORD** that **HE** would deliver him : let **HIM** deliver him, seeing **HE** delighted in him.

9. But **THOU** **ART HE** that took me out of the womb : **THOU** didst make me hope *when* I *was* upon my mother's breasts.

10. I was cast upon **THEE** from the womb: **THOU** art my **GOD** from my mothers belly.

11. Be not far from me ; for trouble is near ; for there is none to help.

12. Many bulls have compassed me : strong *bulls* of Bashan have beset me round.

13. They gaped upon me with their mouths, *as a* raven- -ing and a roaring lion

14. I am poured out like water, and all my bones are out of joint : my heart is like wax ; it is melted in the midst of my bowels.

15. My strength is dried up like a potsherd ; and my ton- -gue cleaveth to my jaws ; and **THOU** hast brought me into the dust of death.

16. For dogs have compassed me : the assembly of the wicked have inclosed me ; they pierced my hands and my feet.

17. I may tell all my bones : they look *and* stare upon me.

18. They part my garments among them, and cast lots upon my vesture.

19. But be not THOU far from me, O LORD: O my strength, haste THEE to help me.

20. Deliver my soul from the sword; my darling from the power of the dog.

21. Save me from the lion's mouth: for THOU hast heard me from the horns of the unicorns.

22. I will declare THY NAME unto my brethren: in the midst of the congregation will I praise THEE.

23. YE THAT FEAR THE LORD, PRAISE HIM; all ye the seed of JACOB glorify HIM; and fear HIM all ye the seed of ISRAEL.

24. For HE hath not despised nor abhorred the affliction of the afflicted; neither hath HE hid HIS FACE from him; but when he cried unto HIM, HE heard.

25. My praise shall be of THEE in the great congregation: I will pay my vows before

them that fear **HIM**.

26. The meek shall eat and be satisfied: they shall **PRAISE THE LORD** that seek **HIM**: your heart shall live for ever.

27. All the ends of the world shall remember and turn un=to the **LORD**: and all the kindreds of the nations shall worship before **THEE**.

28. **FOR THE KINGDOM IS THE LORD'S: AND HE IS THE GOVERNOR AMONG THE NATIONS.**

29. All they that be fat upon earth shall eat and wor=:ship: all they that go down to the dust shall bow before **HIM**: and none can keep alive his own soul.

30. A seed shall serve **HIM**; it shall be accounted to the **LORD** for a generation.

31. They shall come, and shall declare **HIS** righteous=:ness unto a people that shall be born, that **HE** hath done this.

Psalm XXIII

David's confidence in GOD's grace.

A Psalm of David.

The LORD.

is my shepherd; ———
I shall not want.
2. He maketh me to lie
down in green
pastures: He leadeth me beside
the still waters:

3. He restoreth my soul: He leadeth me in the paths of righteousness for His Name's sake.

4. Yea, though I walk through the valley of the shadow of death, I will fear no evil: for THOU art with me; THY rod and THY staff they comfort me.

5. THOU preparest a table be= =fore me in the presence of mine enemies: THOU anoint= =est my head with oil; my cup runneth over.

6. Surely goodness and mercy shall follow me all the days of my life: and I will dwell in the house of the LORD for ever.

Psalm xxiv.

GOD's lordship in the world. The citizens of his spiritual kingdom. An exhortation to receive him.

A Psalm of David.

The earth is the LORD'S, and the

fulness thereof; the world; and they that dwell therein.

2. FOR HE hath founded it upon the seas, and established it upon the floods.

3. WHO shall ascend into the hill of the LORD? or who shall stand in HIS HOLY PLACE?

4. HE that hath clean hands, and a pure heart; who hath not lifted up his soul unto vanity, nor sworn deceitfully.

5. HE shall receive the blessing from the LORD, and righteousness from the GOD of his salvation.

6. THIS is the generation of them that seek HIM, that seek thy face, O Jacob. Selah.

7. LIFT up your heads, O ye gates; and be ye lift up, ye everlasting doors; and the KING OF GLORY shall come in.

8. WHO is this KING OF GLORY? The LORD strong and mighty, the LORD mighty in battle.

9. LIFT up your heads, O ye gates; even lift them up, ye everlasting doors; and the KING OF GLORY shall come in.

10. WHO is this KING OF GLORY? The LORD OF HOSTS, HE is the KING OF GLORY. Selah.

Psalm XXV.

1. David's confid:
:ence in prayer. 7.
He prayeth for
remission of sins, 16
and for help in af:
:fliction. —

A Psalm of
David. —

UNTO THEE,
O LORD, do I lift up my
soul.

2. O my **GOD**, I trust in **THEE**: let
me not be ashamed, let not mine enemies
triumph over me.

3. Yea, let none that wait on **THEE** be ashamed:
let them be ashamed that transgress with:
out cause.

4. Shew me **THY** ways, O LORD; teach
me **THY** paths.

5. Lead me in **THY** truth, and teach me:
for **THOU** art the **GOD OF
MY SALVATION**; on
THEE do I wait all the day.

6. Remember, **O LORD, THY** tender
mercies and **THY** lovingkindnesses;
for they have been ever of old.

7. Remember not the sins of my youth, nor my transgressions: according to THY MERCY remember THOU me for THY goodness' sake O LORD.

8. Good and upright is the **LORD** : therefore will **HE** teach sinners in the way.

9. The meek will **HE** guide in judgement : and the meek will **HE** teach **HIS** way.

10. All the paths of the **LORD** are mercy and truth unto such as keep **HIS** covenant and **HIS** testimonies.

11. For thy name's sake, **O LORD**, pardon mine iniquity; for it is great.

12. What man is he that feareth the **LORD**? him shall **HE** teach in the way that **HE** shall choose.

13 His soul shall dwell at ease; and his seed shall inherit the earth.

14. The secret of the **LORD** is with them that fear **HIM**; and **HE** will shew them **HIS** covenant.

15 Mine eyes are ever toward the **LORD**; for **HE** shall pluck my feet out of the net.

16. Turn **THEE** unto me, and have mercy upon me; for **I** am desolate and afflicted.

17. The troubles of my heart are enlarged: **O**

bring **THOU** me out of my distresses.

18. **L**ook upon mine affliction and my pain; and forgive all my sins.

19. **C**onsider mine enemies; for they are many; and they hate me with cruel hatred.

20. **O** keep my soul, and deliver me: let me not be ashamed; for **I** put my **trust** in **THEE.**

21. **L**et integrity and uprightness preserve me; for **I** wait on **THEE.**

22. **R**edeem **ISRAEL**, **O GOD,** out of all his troubles.

Psalm XXVI.

David resorteth unto **GOD** in confidence of his integrity.
· A · Psalm · of · David ·

JUDGE me, **O LORD**; for **I** have walked in mine integrity: **I** have trusted also in the **LORD**; therefore **I** shall not slide.

2. **Examine me, O Lord**, and prove me; try my reins and my heart.

3. **For THY** lovingkindness is before mine eyes: and I have walked in **THY** truth.

4. **I** have not sat with vain persons, neither will I go in with dissemblers.

5. **I** have hated the congregation of evil doers; and will not sit with the wicked.

6. **I** will wash mine hands in innocency: so will I compass **THINE** altar **O LORD**:

7. **That** I may publish with the voice of thanks=giving, and tell of all **THY** wondrous works.

8. **LORD**, I have loved the habitation of **THY HOUSE**, and the place where **THINE HONOUR** dwelleth.

9. **Gather** not my soul with sinners, nor my life with bloody men.

10. **In** whose hands is mischief, and their right hand is full of bribes.

11. **But** as for me, I will walk in mine in=tegrity: redeem me, and be merci=ful unto me.

12. **My** foot standeth in an even place: in the congregation will I bless the **LORD**.

PSALM

XXVII.

1. David sustaineth his faith by the power of GOD, 4 by his love to the service of GOD, 9 by prayer.

A Psalm of David.

The LORD is my light and my salvation; whom shall

I fear? the LORD is the strength of my life; of whom shall I be afraid?

2. When the wicked, even mine enemies and my foes, came upon me to eat up my flesh, they stumbled and fell.

3. Though an host should encamp against me, my heart shall not fear: though war should rise against me, in this will I be confident.

4. One thing have I desired of the LORD, that will I seek after; that I may dwell in the house of the LORD all the days of my life, to BEHOLD THE BEAUTY OF THE LORD, and to enquire in his temple.

5. For in the time of trouble HE shall hide me in HIS pavilion: in the secret of HIS tabernacle shall HE hide me; HE SHALL set UP UPON A ROCK

6. And now shall mine head be lifted up above mine enemies round about me: therefore will I offer in HIS tabernacle sacrifices of joy; I will sing, yea, I WILL SING PRAISES UNTO THE LORD.

7. Hear, O LORD, when I cry with my voice: have mercy also upon me, and answer me.

8. When thou saidst, Seek ye my face; my heart said unto thee, Thy face, LORD, will I seek.

9. Hide not **THY FACE** far from me; put not **THY** ser=vant away in anger: **THOU HAST BEEN MY HELP; LEAVE ME NOT, NEITHER FORSAKE ME, O GOD OF MY SALVATION.**

10. When my father and my mo=ther forsake me, then the **LORD** will take me up.

11. **TEACH ME THY WAY, O LORD**, and lead me in a plain path, because of mine enemies.

12. Deliver me not over unto the will of mine enemies: for false witnesses are risen up against me, and such as breathe out cruelty.

13. I had fainted, unless I had believed to see the goodness of the **LORD** in the land of the living.

14. **WAIT ON THE LORD: BE OF GOOD COURAGE, AND HE SHALL STRENGTHEN THINE HEART: WAIT, I SAY ON THE**

LORD.

PSALM XXVIII.

1. David prayeth earnestly against his enemies. 6. He blesseth GOD. 9. He prayeth for the people.
A Psalm of David.

UNTO THEE will I cry O LORD my rock; be not silent to me: lest, if THOU be silent to me, I become like them that go down into the pit.

2. HEAR the voice of my supplications, when I cry unto THEE, when I lift up my hands toward THY holy temple.

3. DRAW me not away with the wicked, and with the workers of iniquity, which speak peace to their neighbours, but mischief is in their hearts.

4. GIVE them according to their deeds, and according to the wickedness of their endeavours: give them after the works of their hands; render to them their desert.

5. BECAUSE they regard not the works of the LORD, nor the operation of HIS HANDS, HE shall destroy them, and not build them up.

6. Blessed be the LORD, because HE hath heard the voice of my supplication.

7. The LORD is my strength and my shield; my heart trusted in HIM, and I am helped: therefore my heart greatly rejoiceth; and with my song will I praise HIM.

8. The LORD is their strength, and HE is the saving strength of HIS people.

9. SAVE THY people, and bless THINE inheritance: Feed them also, and lift them up for ever.

✳ NAZARETH ✳ FROM ✳ ABOVE ✳ THE ✳ WELL. ✳

PSALM XXIX.

1. David exhorteth princes to give glory to GOD,
3. by reason of His power, 11. and protection of
His people.   A Psalm of David.

GIVE unto the LORD, O ye mighty, give unto the LORD glory and strength.

2. Give unto the LORD the glory due unto HIS NAME; worship the LORD in the beauty of Holiness.

3. The voice of the LORD is upon the waters; the GOD of Glory thundereth: the Lord is upon many waters.

4. The voice of the LORD is powerful; the voice of the LORD is full of majesty.

5. The voice of the LORD breaketh the cedars; yea, the LORD breaketh the cedars of Lebanon.

6. He maketh them also to skip like a calf; Lebanon and Sirion like a young unicorn.

7. The voice of the LORD divideth the flames of fire.

8. The voice of the LORD shak-=eth the wilderness;

the **LORD** shaketh the wilderness of **Kadesh**.

9. The voice of the **LORD** maketh the hinds to calve, and discovereth the forests: and in **His** temple doth every one speak of **His** glory.

10. The **LORD** sitteth upon the flood; yea, the **LORD** sitteth King for ever.

11. The **LORD** will give strength unto **His** people; the LORD will bless **HIS** people with peace.

PSALM XXX

1. David praiseth **GOD** for his deliverance.
4. He exhorteth others to praise **HIM** by example of **GOD'S** dealing with him. A Psalm and Song at the dedication of the house of David.

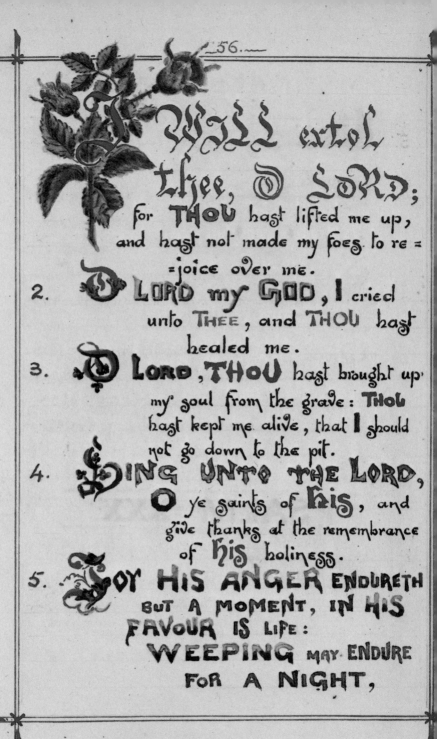

I WILL extol thee, O LORD; for THOU hast lifted me up, and hast not made my foes to rejoice over me.

2. O LORD my GOD, I cried unto THEE, and THOU hast healed me.

3. O LORD, THOU hast brought up my soul from the grave: THOU hast kept me alive, that I should not go down to the pit.

4. SING UNTO THE LORD, O ye saints of his, and give thanks at the remembrance of his holiness.

5. FOR HIS ANGER ENDURETH BUT A MOMENT, IN HIS FAVOUR IS LIFE: WEEPING MAY ENDURE FOR A NIGHT,

BUT JOY COMETH IN THE MORNING.

6. AND in my prosperity I said, I shall never be moved.

7. LORD, by thy favour thou hast made my mountain to stand strong: thou didst hide thy face, and I was troubled.

8. I cried to thee, O LORD; and unto the LORD I made supplication.

9. WHAT profit is there in my blood, when I go down to the pit? Shall the dust praise thee? shall it declare thy truth?

10. HEAR, O LORD, AND HAVE MERCY UPON ME: LORD, BE THOU MY HELPER.

11. THOU hast turned for me my mourning into dancing: Thou hast put off my sackcloth, and girded me with gladness;

~58.~

To the end that my glory may sing praise to thee, and not be silent. O LORD MY GOD, I will give thanks unto THEE for ever.

PSALM XXXI.

1. David shewing his confidence in GOD craveth His help. 7. He rejoiceth in His mercy. 9. He prayeth in his calamity. 19. He praiseth GOD for His goodness.

To the chief Musician, A Psalm of David.

IN THEE, O LORD, do I put my trust; let me never be ashamed: deliver me in thy righteousness.

2. BOW down thine ear to me; deliver me speedily: be thou my strong rock, for an house of defence to save me.

3. FOR thou art my rock and my fortress;

therefore for **thy** name's sake lead me,
and guide me.

4. **PULL** me out of the net that they have laid pri=
=vily for me: for **thou** art my strength.

5. **INTO THY HAND I COMMIT
MY SPIRIT:**
thou hast redeemed me, **O LORD
GOD** of truth.

6. **I** have hated them that regard lying vanities: but **I**
trust in the **LORD.**

7. **I** will be glad and rejoice in **thy** mercy: for **thou**
hast considered my trouble; **thou** hast
known my soul in adversities;

8. **AND** hast not shut me up into the hand of
the enemy: **thou** hast set my feet in
a large room.

9. **HAVE** mercy upon me, **O LORD**, for **I** am
in trouble: mine eye is consumed with
grief, yea, my soul and my belly.

10. **FOR** my life is spent with grief, and my years
with sighing: my strength faileth be=
=cause of mine iniquity, and my bones
are consumed.

11. **I** was a reproach among all mine enemies,
but especially among my neighbours,

and a fear to mine acquaintance: they that did see me without fled from me.

12. I am forgotten as a dead man out of mind: I am like a broken vessel.

13. FOR I have heard the slander of many: fear was on every side: while they took counsel together against me, they devised to take away my life.

14. BUT I trusted in thee, O LORD: I said, Thou art my GOD.

15. MY times are in thy hand: deliver me from the hand of my enemies, and from them that persecute me.

16. MAKE thy face to shine upon thy servant: save me for thy mercies' sake.

17. LET me not be ashamed, O LORD; for I have called upon thee: let the wicked be ashamed, and let them be silent in the grave.

18. LET the lying lips be put to silence; which speak grievous things proudly and contemptuously against the righteous.

19. OH how great is thy goodness, which thou hast laid up for them that fear thee; which thou hast wrought for them that trust in thee before the sons of men!

20. Thou shalt hide them in the secret of thy presence

From the pride of man: **thou** shalt keep them secretly in a pavilion from the strife of tongues.

21. Blessed be the Lord: for **He hath shewed** me **His marvellous kindness** in a strong city.

22. For I said in my haste, I am cut off from before **thine** eyes: nevertheless **thou** heardest the voice of my supplications when I cried unto **thee**

23. O love the **Lord**, all ye **His** saints: for the **Lord** preserveth the faithful, and plentifully rewardeth the proud doer.

24. Be of good courage, and He shall strengthen your heart, all ye that hope in the **Lord.**

PSALM XXXII.

1. Blessedness consisteth in remiss=tion of sins. 3. Confession of sins giveth ease to the conscience. 8. GOD'S promises giveth joy. A Psalm of David, Maschil.

BLESSED is he whose trans=gression is forgiven, whose sin is covered.

2. Blessed is the man unto whom the **LORD** imputeth not iniquity, and in whose spirit there is no guile.

3. When I kept silence, my bones waxed old through my roaring all the day long.

4. For day and night **Thy** hand was heavy upon me: my moisture is turned into the drought of summer. **Selah.**

5. I acknowledged my sin unto **Thee**, and mine ini=quity have I not hid. I said, I will con=fess my transgressions unto the **LORD**; and **Thou** forgavest the iniquity of my sin. **Selah.**

6. For this shall every one that is godly pray unto **Thee** in a time when **Thou** mayest be found: surely in the floods of great waters they shall not come nigh

unto **Him.**

7. **Thou** art my hiding place; **Thou** shalt preserve me from trouble; **Thou** shalt compass me about with songs of deliverance. **Selah.**

8. I will instruct thee and teach thee in the way which thou shalt go: **I will guide thee with Mine eye.**

9. Be ye not as the horse, or as the mule, which have no understanding: whose mouth must be held in with bit and bridle, lest they come near unto thee.

10. Many sorrows shall be to the wicked: but he that trusteth in the **LORD**, mercy shall compass him about.

11. Be glad in the **Lord**, and rejoice, ye righteous: and shout for joy, all ye that are upright in heart.

PSALM XXXIII.

1. **GOD** is to be praised for His goodness, 6. for His power, 12. and for His providence. 20. Confidence is to be placed in **GOD**.

REJOICE in the LORD, O ye righteous: for praise is comely for the upright.

2. Praise the LORD with harp: sing unto him with the psaltery and an instrument of ten strings.

3. Sing unto him a new song; play skilfully with a loud noise.

4. For the word of the LORD is right; and all his works are done in truth.

5. He loveth righteousness and judgement: the earth is full of the goodness of the LORD.

6. By the word of the LORD were the heavens made; and all the host of them by the breath of his mouth.

7. He gathered the waters of the sea together as an heap: he layeth up the depth in storehouses.

8. Let all the earth fear the LORD: let all the inhabitants of the world stand in awe of him.

9. For he spake, and it was done; he commanded, and it stood fast.

10. The LORD bringeth the counsel of the heathen to nought: he maketh the devices of the people of none effect.

11. The counsel of the LORD standeth for ever, the thoughts of his heart to all generations.

12. Blessed is the nation whose GOD is the LORD; and the people whom he hath chosen for his own inheritance.

13. The LORD looketh from heaven; he beholdeth all the sons of men.

14. From the place of his habitation he looketh upon all the inhabitants of the earth.

15. He fashioneth their hearts alike; he considereth all their works.

16. There is no king saved by the multitude of an host: a mighty man is not delivered by much strength.

17. An horse is a vain thing for safety: neither shall he deliver any by his great strength.

18. Behold, the eye of the LORD is upon them that fear him, upon them that hope in His mercy.

19. To deliver their soul from death, and to keep them alive in famine.

20. Our soul waiteth for the LORD : he is our help and our shield.

21. For our heart shall rejoice in him, because we have trusted in His holy name.

22. Let thy mercy, O LORD, be upon us, according as we hope in thee.

Psalm XXXIV.

1. David praiseth GOD, and exhorteth others thereto by his experience. 8. They are blessed that trust in GOD. 11. He exhorteth to the fear of GOD. 15. The privileges of the righteous.
A Psalm of David, when he changed his behaviour before Abimelech, who drove him away, and he departed.

I WILL bless the LORD at all times: his praise shall continually be in my mouth.

2. My soul shall make her boast in the LORD : the humble shall hear thereof, and be glad.

3. O magnify the LORD with me, and let us exalt his name together.

4. I sought the LORD, and he heard me, and delivered me from all my fears.

5. They looked unto him, and were lightened; and

their faces were not ashamed.

6. The poor man cried, and the **LORD** heard him, saved him out of all his troubles.

7. The **ANGEL of the LORD** encampeth round about them that fear him, and delivereth them.

8. O taste and see that the **LORD** is good: blessed is the man that trusteth in **HIM.**

9. O fear the **LORD**, ye his saints: for there is no want to them that fear him.

10. The young lions do lack, and suffer hunger: but they that seek the **LORD** shall not want any good thing

11. Come, ye children, hearken unto me: I will teach you the fear of the **LORD.**

12. What man is he that desireth life, and loveth many days, that he may see good?

13. KEEP THY TONGUE FROM EVIL, AND THY LIPS FROM SPEAKING GUILE.

14. Depart from evil, and do good; seek peace, and pursue it.

15. The eyes of the **LORD** are upon the righteous, and **his** ears are open unto their cry.

16. The face of the **LORD** is against them that do evil, to cut off the remembrance of them from the earth.

17. The righteous cry, and the **LORD** heareth, and de= =delivereth them out of all their troubles.

18. The LORD is nigh unto them that are of a broken heart; and saveth such as be of a contrite spirit.

19. Many are the afflictions of the righteous: But the **LORD** delivereth him out of them all.

20. HE keepeth all his bones : not one of them is bro= =ken.

21. Evil shall slay the wicked : and they that hate the righteous shall be desolate.

22. The **LORD** redeemeth the soul of his ser= =vants : and none of them that trust in him shall be desolate.

PSALM XXXV.

1. David prayeth for his own safety, and his enemies' confusion. 11. He
complaineth of their wrongful dealing.
22. Thereby he
inciteth GOD against them.
A Psalm of David.

Plead my cause,
O LORD,
with them that
strive with me:
fight
against them
that fight
against me.

2. Take
hold of shield and buckler,
and stand up for mine
help.
3. Draw out also the
spear, and stop the way
against them that persecute
me: say unto my
soul, I am thy
salvation.
4. Let them be confounded
and put to shame that

seek after my soul : let them be turned back and brought to confusion that devise my hurt.

5. **Let** them be as chaff before the wind : and let the **angel of the Lord** chase them.

6. **Let** their way be dark and slippery : and let the **angel of the Lord** persecute them.

7. **For** without cause have they hid for me their net in a pit, which without cause they have digged for my soul.

8. **Let** destruction come upon him at unawares ; and let his net that he hath hid catch himself : into that very destruc= =tion let him fall.

9. **And** my soul shall be joyful in the **Lord** : it shall rejoice in **His salvation.**

10. **All** my bones shall say, **Lord**, who is like unto **Thee**, which deliverest the poor from him that is too strong for him, yea, the poor and the needy from him that spoileth him.

11. **False** witnesses did rise up ; they laid to my charge things that I knew not.

12. **They** rewarded me evil for good to the spoiling of my soul.

13. **But** as for me, when they were sick, my clothing was sackcloth ; I humbled my soul with fasting ; and my prayer returned into mine own bosom.

14. **I** behaved myself as though he had been my friend or brother : I bowed down heavily, as one that

mourneth for his mother.

15. **But** in mine adversity they rejoiced, and gathered them=
=selves together: yea, the abjects gathered them=
=selves together against me, and I knew it not;
they did tear me, and ceased not:

16. **With** hypocritical mockers in feasts, they gnashed
upon me with their teeth.

17. **Lord**, how long wilt **Thou** look on? rescue
my soul from their destructions, my darling
from the lions.

18. **I** will give **Thee** thanks in the great congregation:
I will praise **Thee** among much people.

19. **Let** not them that are mine enemies wrongfully re=
=joice over me: neither let them wink with
the eye that hate me without a cause.

20. **For** they speak not peace: but they devise de=
=ceitful matters against them that are quiet
in the land.

21. **Yea**, they opened their mouth wide against me,
and said, **Aha**, aha, our eye hath seen it.

22. **This Thou** hast seen, **O Lord**:
keep not silence: **O Lord**, be not far
from me.

23. **Stir** up **Thyself**, and awake to my judg=
=ment, even unto my cause, my **God**
and my **Lord**.

24. **Judge** me, **O Lord** my **God**,
according to **Thy** righteousness;
and let them not rejoice over me.

25. **Let** them not say in their hearts, **Ah,** so would we have it : let them not say, **We** have swal= =lowed him up.

26. **Let** them be ashamed and brought to confusion together that rejoice at mine hurt: let them be clothed with shame and dishonour that magnify themselves against me.

27. **Let** them shout for joy, and be glad, that favour my righteous cause : yea, let them say continually, **LET THE LORD BE MAGNIFIED**, which hath pleasure in the prosperity of **HIS** servant.

28. **And** my tongue shall speak of **THY** right= =eousness and of **THY** praise all the day long.

Psalm XXXVI.

1. The grievous estate of the wicked.
5. The excellency of God's mercy.
10. David prayeth for favour to God's children.

To the Chief Musician, A Psalm of David, the servant of the **LORD.**

THE transgression of the wick=
=ed saith within my heart, that
there is no fear of **GOD** before
his eyes.

2. **For** he flattereth himself in his
own eyes, until his iniquity be found to be
hateful.

3. **The** words of his mouth are iniquity and de=
=ceit: he hath left off to be wise, and
to do good.

4. **He** deviseth mischief upon his bed; he
setteth himself in a way that is
not good; he abhorreth not evil.

5. **THY MERCY, O
LORD, IS IN THE
HEAVENS; and
THY Faithfulness
reacheth unto the
clouds.**

6. **THY** right=
=eousness is like
the great mountains;
THY judgments are
a great deep:
O LORD, THOU pre=
=servest man and beast.

7. **HOW EXCELLENT** is **THY
LOVINGKINDNESS,
O GOD!**
therefore the children of men put their trust
under the shadow of **THY** wings.
8. **THEY** shall be abundantly satisfied with
the fatness of **THY** house; and
THOU shalt make them drink of
the river of **THY** pleasures.

9. For with **THEE** is the foun=
=tain of life:

in **thy** light shall we see light.

10. **O** continue **thy** lovingkindness unto them that know **thee**; and **thy** right=
=eousness to the upright in heart.

11. **Let** not the foot of pride come against me, and let not the hand of the wicked remove me.

12. **There** are the workers of iniquity fallen: they are cast down, and shall not be able to rise.

PSALM XXXVII.

*David persuaded to patience and confidence in God, by the different es-
tate of the godly and the wicked.
A Psalm of David.*

FRET not thyself because of evildoers, neither be thou envious against the workers of iniquity.

2. **For** they shall soon be cut down like the grass, and wither as the green herb.

3. **Trust in the LORD, and do good;**

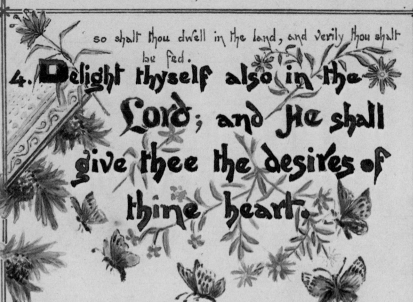

so shalt thou dwell in the land, and verily thou shalt be fed.

4. Delight thyself also in the Lord; and He shall give thee the desires of thine heart.

WEST END OF CARMEL WITH THE MONASTERY.

5. **Commit thy way un-to the Lord; trust also in HIM; and HE shall bring it to pass.**

6. **And HE** shall bring forth thy righteousness as the light, and **THY** judgment as the noonday.

7. **REST IN THE LORD,** and wait patiently for **HIM:** fret not thyself because of him who prospereth in his way, because of the man who bringeth wicked devices to pass.

8. **CEASE FROM ANGER, AND FORSAKE WRATH: FRET NOT THYSELF IN ANY WISE TO DO EVIL.**

9. **FOR EVILDOERS SHALL BE CUT OFF: BUT THOSE THAT WAIT UPON THE LORD, THEY SHALL INHERIT THE EARTH.**

10. **For** yet a little while, and the wicked shall not be: yea, thou shalt diligently consider his place, and it shall not be.

11. **But** the meek shall inherit the earth;

RACHEL'S TOMB IN THE WAY TO EPHRATH, WHICH IS BETHLEHEM.

and shall delight themselves in the abundance of peace.

12. **The** wicked plotteth against the just, and gnasheth upon him with his teeth.

13. **The Lord** shall laugh at him: for **HE** seeth that his day is coming.

14. **The** wicked have drawn out the sword, and have bent their bow, to cast down the poor and needy, and to slay such as be of upright conversation.

15. **Their** sword shall enter into their own heart, and their bows shall be broken.

16. **A** little that a righteous man hath is better than the riches of many wicked.

17. **For** the arms of the wicked shall be broken: but **the LORD upholdeth the righteous.**

18. **The LORD** knoweth the days of the upright: and their inheritance shall be for ever.

19. **They** shall not be ashamed in the evil time: and in the days of famine they shall be satisfied.

20. **But** the wicked shall perish, and the enemies of the **LORD** shall be as the fat of lambs: they shall consume; into smoke shall they consume away.

21. **The** wicked borroweth, and payeth not again: but the righteous sheweth mercy, and giveth.

22. **For** such as be blessed of **HIM** shall inherit the earth; and they that be cursed of **HIM** shall be cut off.

23. **The steps of a good man are ordered by the LORD:** and **HE** delighteth in his way.

24. **Though** he fall, he shall not be utterly cast down: for the **LORD** upholdeth him with **HIS** hand.

25. **I HAVE BEEN YOUNG, AND NOW AM OLD; YET HAVE I NOT SEEN THE RIGHTEOUS FORSAKEN, NOR HIS SEED BEGGING BREAD.—**

SIDON; AND THE ANCIENT CASTLE.

26. HE is ever merciful, and lendeth; and his seed is blessed.

27. Depart from evil, and do good; and dwell for evermore.

28. For the LORD loveth judgment, and for=saketh not his saints; they are pre=served for ever: but the seed of the wicked shall be cut off.

29. The righteous shall inherit the land, and dwell therein for ever.

30. The mouth of the righteous speaketh wisdom, and his tongue talketh of judgment.

31. The law of his God is in his heart; none of steps shall slide.

32. The wicked watcheth the righteous, and seeketh to slay him.

33. The Lord will not leave him in his hand, nor condemn him when he is judged.

34. Wait on the LORD, and keep His way, and HE shall exalt thee to inherit the land: when the wicked are cut off, thou shalt see it.

35. I have seen the wicked in great power, and spreading himself like a green bay tree.

36. Yet he passed away, and, lo, he was not: yea, I sought him, but he could not be found.

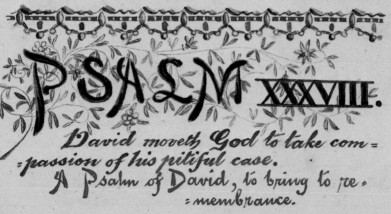

37. MARK THE PERFECT MAN, AND BEHOLD THE UPRIGHT: FOR THE END OF THAT MAN IS PEACE.

38. But the transgressors shall be destroyed together: the end of the wicked shall be cut off.

39. But the salvation of the righteous is of the LORD: HE is their strength in the time of trouble.

40. And the LORD shall help them, and deliver them: HE shall deliver them from the wicked, and save them, because they trust in HIM.

PSALM XXXVIII.

David moveth God to take com=
=passion of his pitiful case.
A Psalm of David, to bring to re=
=membrance.

 **LORD,**

rebuke me not in THY wrath: neither chas:ten me in THY hot displeasure.

2. For THINE arrows stick fast in me, and THY hand presseth me sore.

THE WATCH TOWER,
THEBEN
ON THE DANUBE.

3. **There** is no sound:
=ness in my flesh because of
THINE anger; neither is
there any rest in my bones because
of my sin.......

4. **For** mine iniquities are gone over mine head: as an heavy
burden they are too heavy for me.

5. **My** wounds stink and are corrupt because of my foolishness.

6. I am troubled; I am bowed down greatly; I go
mourning all the day long.

7. **For** my loins are filled with a loathsome disease:

and there is no soundness in my flesh.

8. I am feeble and sore broken: I have roared by rea=
son of the disquietness of my heart.

9. LORD, all my desire is before Thee; and my
groaning is not hid from Thee.

10. My heart panteth, my strength faileth me: as
for the light of mine eyes, it also is gone
from me.

11. My lovers and my friends stand aloof from my
sore; and my kinsmen stand afar off.

12. They also that seek after my life lay snares for me:
and they that seek my hurt speak mischievous
things, and imagine deceits all the day long.

13. But I, as a deaf man, heard not; and I was
as a dumb man that openeth not his mouth.

14. Thus I was as a man that heareth not, and
in whose mouth are no reproofs.

15. For in Thee, O Lord,
do I hope: Thou
wilt hear, O Lord
my God.

16. For I said, Hear me, lest otherwise they
should rejoice over me: when my foot slip=
=peth, they magnify themselves against me.

VISEGRAD,—
 (IN HUNGARY) — ON THE DANUBE.

17. FOR I am ready to halt, and my sorrow is
        continually before me.
18. For I will declare mine iniquity; I will be
        sorry for my sin.
19. But mine enemies are lively, and they are
        strong: and they that hate me wrongfully
        are multiplied.
20. They also that render evil for good are mine
        adversaries; because I follow the thing
        that good is.
21. FORSAKE ME NOT, O LORD:
    O MY GOD, BE NOT FAR
        FROM ME.

22. Make haste to help me,
O Lord my salvation.

PSALM XXXIX.

1. David's care of his thoughts. 4. The consideration of the brevity and vanity of life, the reverence of God's judg= =ments, 10 and prayer, are his bri= =dles of impatiency.

To the chief Musician, even to Jedu= =thun, A Psalm of David.

I SAID, I will take heed to my ways, that I sin not with my tongue: I will keep my mouth with a bridle, while the wicked is before me.

2. I was dumb with silence, I held my peace, even from good; and my sorrow was stirred.

3. My heart was hot within me, while I was musing the fire burned: then spake I with my tongue.

4. LORD, MAKE ME TO KNOW MINE

END; AND THE MEASURE OF
MY DAYS; WHAT IT IS; THAT
I MAY KNOW HOW FRAIL I AM:

5. BEHOLD, THOU hast made my days as an hand:
breadth; and mine age is as nothing before
THEE: verily every man at his best state
is altogether vanity. Selah.

6. SURELY every man walketh in a vain shew:
surely they are disquieted in vain: he heap:
:eth up riches, and knoweth not who shall
gather them.

7. AND now, LORD, what wait
I for? my hope is in
THEE.

8. DELIVER me from all my transgressions: make
me not the reproach of the foolish.

9. I was dumb, I opened not my mouth; because
THOU didst it.

10. REMOVE THY stroke away from me: I am
consumed by the blow of THINE hand.

11. WHEN THOU with rebukes dost correct man
for iniquity, THOU makest his beauty to con:
:sume away like a moth: SURELY EVERY
MAN IS VANITY. Selah.

12. HEAR MY PRAYER, O LORD,
and give ear unto my
cry; hold not THY peace at my tears:
for I am a stranger with THEE, and a
sojourner, as all my fathers were.

13. **O** spare me, that **I** may recover strength, before **I** go hence, and be no more.

Psalm XL.

1. The benefit of confidence in **GOD**.
6. Obedience is the best sacrifice. 11. The sense of **David's** evils inflameth his prayer.

To the chief Musician, A Psalm of David.

I WAITED patiently for the **LORD**; and **HE** inclined unto me, and heard my cry.
2. **HE** brought me up also out of an horrible pit, out of the miry clay, and **SET MY FEET UPON A ROCK**, and **ESTABLISHED MY GOINGS**.
3. **AND HE HATH PUT A NEW SONG IN MY MOUTH, EVEN PRAISE UNTO OUR GOD**: many shall see it, and fear, and shall trust in the **Lord**.

4. Blessed is that man that maketh the Lord his trust, and respecteth not the proud, nor such as turn aside to lies.

MANY, O Lord my God, are thy wonder- -ful works which thou hast done, and thy thoughts which are to us-ward: they cannot be reckoned up in order unto THEE: if I would de- -clare and speak of them, they are more than can be numbered.

6. **Sacrifice** and offering thou didst not desire; mine ears hast thou opened: burnt offering and sin offering hast thou not required.

7. **Then** said I, Lo I come: in the volume of the book it is written of me,

8. **I DELIGHT TO DO THY WILL, O MY GOD:**

9. **I** have preached righteousness in the great congre=gation: lo, I have not refrained my lips, **O Lord, thou** knowest.

10. I have not hid **Thy righteousness** within my heart; I have declared **Thy faithfulness** and **Thy salvation:** I have not concealed **Thy lovingkindness** and **Thy truth** from the great congregation.

11. Withhold not thy tender mercies from me, O LORD: let thy lovingkindness and thy truth continually preserve me.

12. For innumerable evils have compassed me about, mine iniquities have taken hold upon me, so that I am not able to look up; they are more than the hairs of mine head: therefore my heart faileth me.

13. Be pleased, O LORD, to deliver me: O LORD, make haste to help me.

14. Let them be ashamed and confounded together that seek after my soul to destroy it; let them be driven backward and put to shame that wish me evil.

15. Let them be desolate for a reward of their shame that say unto me, Aha, aha.

16. Let all those that seek thee rejoice and be glad in thee: let such as love thy salvation say continually,

The Lord be magnified.

17. But I am poor and needy; yet the LORD thinketh upon me: thou art my help and my deliverer; make no tarrying, O my God.

Psalm XLI.

1. GOD'S care of the poor. 4. David complain=eth of his enemies' treachery. 10. He fleeth to GOD for succour.

To the chief Musician, A Psalm of David.

BLESSED is he that con=sidereth the poor: the LORD will de=liver him in time of trouble.

2. THE LORD will preserve him, and keep him alive; and he shall be blessed upon the earth: and THOU wilt not deliver him unto the will of his enemies.

3. THE LORD will strengthen him upon the bed of languishing: THOU wilt make all his bed in his sickness.

4. I SAID, LORD, be merciful unto me: heal my soul; for I have sinned against thee.

5. MINE enemies speak evil of me, When shall he die, and his name perish?

6. **AND** if he come to see me, he speaketh vanity: his heart gathereth iniquity to itself; when he goeth abroad, he telleth it.

7. **All** that hate me whisper together against me: against me do they devise my hurt.

8. **An** evil disease, say they, cleaveth fast unto him: and now that he lieth he shall rise up no more.

9. **Yea**, mine own familiar friend, in whom I trusted, which did eat of my bread, hath lifted up his heel against me.

10. **But THOU, O LORD**, be merciful unto me, and raise me up, that I may re= =quite them.

11. **By** this I know that **thou** favourest me, because mine enemy doth not triumph over me.

12. **And** as for me, **thou** upholdest me in mine integrity, and settest me before **thy face** for ever.

13. **Blessed be the LORD GOD of ISRAEL from everlasting, and to everlasting. Amen, and Amen.**

PSALM XLIII.

1. David's zeal to serve GOD in the temple.
3. He encourageth his soul to trust in GOD.

To the chief Musician, Maschil, for the sons of Korah

AS THE HART PANTETH AFTER THE WATER BROOKS, SO PANTETH MY SOUL AFTER THEE ☩ GOD.

2 **MY SOUL THIRSTETH FOR GOD, FOR THE LIVING GOD: When shall I come and appear before God?**

3. **MY** tears have been my meat day and night, while they continually say unto me, **Where is thy GOD?**

4. **WHEN I** remember these things, I pour out my soul in me: for I had gone with the multitude, I went with them to the house of **GOD**, with the voice of joy and praise, with a multitude that kept holyday.

5. **WHY** art thou cast down, O my soul? and why art thou disquieted in me? hope thou in **GOD**: for I will yet praise **HIM** for the help of **HIS** countenance.

6. **O** my **GOD**, my soul is cast down within me: therefore will **I** remember **THEE** from the land of Jordan, and of the Hermonites, from the hill **Mizar**.

7. **Deep** calleth unto deep at the noise of **THY** waterspouts; all **THY** waves and **THY** billows are gone over me.

8. **Y**et the **LORD** will command **HIS** loving-kindness in the daytime, and in the night **HIS** song shall be with me, and my prayer unto the **GOD** of my life.

9. I WILL SAY UNTO GOD MY ROCK, WHY HAST THOU FORGOTTEN ME? why go I mourning because of the oppression of the enemy?

10. AS with a SWORD in my bones, mine enemies reproach me; while they say daily unto me, Where is thy GOD?

11. WHY ART THOU CAST DOWN, O MY SOUL? AND WHY ART THOU DISQUIETED WITHIN ME? HOPE THOU IN GOD: FOR I SHALL YET PRAISE HIM, WHO IS THE HEALTH OF MY COUNTENANCE AND MY GOD.

PSALM XLIII.

1. David; praying to be restored to the temple, promiseth to serve GOD joyfully: 5. He encourageth his soul to trust in GOD.

JUDGE me, O GOD, and plead my cause against an ungodly nation: O deliver me from the deceitful and unjust man.

2. For THOU art the GOD of my Strength: why dost THOU cast me off? why go I mourning because of the oppression of the enemy?

3. O send out THY·LIGHT and THY TRUTH: let them lead me; let them bring me unto THY HOLY HILL, and to THY TABERNACLES.

4. Then will I go unto the ALTAR of GOD, unto GOD my exceeding joy: yea, upon the harp will I praise THEE,

O GOD MY GOD.

5. Why art thou cast down O my soul ?
and why art thou disquieted within me?

HOPE IN GOD :

for I shall yet praise HIM,

VVHO IS THE HEALTH

OF MY COUNTENANCE

AND MY GOD.

PSALM XLIV.

1. The church, in memory of former fav=
=ours, 7. complaineth of their present evils.
17. Professing her integrity, 23. she fer=
=vently prayeth for succour.

To the chief Musician for the sons of Korah,
Maschil.

WE have heard with our ears, O GOD, our fathers have told us, what work THOU didst in their days, in the times of old.

2. How Thou didst drive out the heathen with THY hand, and plantedst them; how THOU didst afflict the people, and cast them out.

3. FOR they got not the land in possession by their own sword, neither did their own arm save them: but THY RIGHT HAND, and THINE ARM, and the LIGHT of THY COUNTENANCE, because THOU hadst a favour unto them.

4. THOU art my KING, O GOD: command deliverance for JACOB.

5. Through thee will we push down our enemies: through thy name will we tread them under that rise up a=
=gainst us.

6. For I will not trust in my bow, neither shall my sword save me.

7. But thou hast saved us from our enemies, and hast put them to shame that hated us.

8. In GOD we boast all the day long, and praise THY NAME for ever. Selah.

9. But thou hast cast off; and put us to shame; and goest not forth with our armies.

10. **THOU** makest us to turn back from the enemy: and they which hate us spoil for themselves.

11. **THOU** hast given us like sheep appointed for meat; and hast scattered us among the heathen.

12. **THOU** sellest **THY** people for not, and dost not in=:crease **THY** wealth by their price.

13. **THOU** makest us a reproach to our neighbours, a scorn and a derision to them that are round about us.

14. **THOU** makest us a byword among the heathen, a shaking of the head among the people.

15. **MY** confusion is continually before me, and the shame of my face hath covered me,

16. **FOR** the voice of him that reproacheth and blasphemeth; by reason of the enemy and the avenger.

17. **ALL** this is come upon us, yet have we not forgotten **THEE** neither have we dealt falsely in **thy** covenant.

18. **OUR** heart is not turned back, neither have our steps declined from **thy** way;

19. **THOUGH THOU** hast sore broken us in the place of dragons, and covered us with the shadow of death.

20. **IF** we have forgotten the name of our **GOD**, or stretch=:ed out our hands to a strange god;

21. **SHALL** not **GOD** search this out? for **HE** knoweth the secrets of the heart.

22. **YEA**, for **THY SAKE** are we killed all the day long; we are counted as sheep for the slaughter.

23. **ARISE, WHY SLEEPEST THOU, O LORD?** arise, cast us not off for ever.

24. WHEREFORE hidest THOU THY face, and forgettest our affliction and our oppression?

25. FOR our soul is bowed down to the dust: our belly cleaveth unto the earth.

26. ARISE FOR OUR HELP, AND REDEEM US FOR THY MERCIES' SAKE.

PSALM XLV.

1. The majesty and grace of Christ's kingdom. 10. The duty of the church, and the benefits thereof.

To the chief Musician upon Shoshannim, for the sons of Korah, Maschil, A Song of loves.

MY HEART is inditing a good matter: I speak of the things which have made touching the king: my tongue is the pen of a ready writer.

2. THOU art fairer than the children of men: grace is poured into thy lips: therefore GOD hath blessed thee for ever.

3. **GIRD** thy sword upon thy thigh, O most mighty, with thy glory and thy majesty.

4. **AND** in thy majesty ride prosperously because of truth and meekness and righteousness; and thy right hand shall teach thee terrible things.

5. **THINE** arrows are sharp in the heart of the king's enemies; whereby the people fall under thee.

6. **THY THRONE, O GOD, IS FOR EVER AND EVER: ✠ THE SCEPTRE OF THY KINGDOM IS A RIGHT SCEPTRE.**

7. **THOU** lovest **RIGHTEOUSNESS**, and hatest wickedness: therefore **GOD**, thy **GOD**, hath anointed thee with the oil of gladness above thy fellows.

8. **ALL** thy garments smell of
myrrh, and **ALOES,**
and cassia, out of the ivory
palaces, whereby they have
made thee glad.
9. **KINGS'** daughters were
among thy honourable women:
upon thy right hand did stand the queen
in gold of Ophir.
10. **HEARKEN**, O daughter, and
consider, and incline thine ear; forget
also thine own people, and thy fa-
-ther's house.
11. **So** shall the **KING** greatly
desire thy beauty: for
HE is thy **LORD**; and wor-
-ship thou **HIM.**
12. **AND** the daughter of **TYRE** shall be
there with a gift; even the rich
among the people shall intreat
thy favour.
13. **THE** king's daughter is all
glorious within:
her clothing is of
wrought gold.

TYRE.

14. **SHE** shall be brought unto the king
in raiment of needlework: the
virgins her companions that fol-
=low her shall be brought unto
thee.

15. **WITH** gladness and rejoicing shall they be brought:
they shall enter into the king's palace.

16. **INSTEAD** of thy fathers shall be thy children, whom
thou mayest make princes in all the earth.

17. **I** will make thy name to be remembered in all gen=
=erations: therefore shall the people praise
thee for ever and ever.

PSALM XLVI.

1. The confidence which the church hath in GOD. 8. An exhorta-
tion to behold it.
To the chief Musician for the sons of
Korah, ᴧᴧᴧᴧᴧA. Song upon Alamoth.

GOD IS OUR REFUGE AND STRENGTH, A·VERY·PRESENT·HELP·IN·TROUBLE.

2. THEREFORE WILL NOT WE FEAR
THOUGH THE EARTH BE REMOVED,
AND THOUGH THE MOUNTAINS
BE CARRIED INTO THE MIDST
OF THE SEA.

3. Though the waters thereof roar
and be troubled, though the mountains shake with the swelling
thereof. SELAH.

4. THERE IS A RIVER, THE STREAMS WHERE OF SHALL MAKE GLAD THE CITY OF GOD, THE HOLY PLACE OF THE TABERNACLES OF THE MOST HIGH.

5. GOD is in the midst of her; she shall not be moved: GOD shall help her, and that right early.

6. The heathen raged, the kingdoms were moved, HE uttered HIS voice, the earth melted.

7. The LORD of HOSTS is with us; the GOD of JACOB IS OUR REFUGE. Selah.

8. Come, behold the works of the LORD, what desolations HE hath made in the earth.

9. HE maketh wars to cease unto the end of the earth; HE breaketh the bow, and cutteth the spear in sunder; HE burneth the cha=riot in the fire.

10. Be still, and know that I am God: I will be exalted among the heathen; I will be exalted in the earth.

11. THE LORD of HOSTS IS WITH US; THE God of JACOB IS OUR REFUGE. Selah.

PSALM XLVII.

The nations are exhorted cheerfully to en-
:tertain the kingdom of Christ.
To the chief Musician, A Psalm for the sons of Korah.

O CLAP your hands, all ye people; shout
unto GOD with the voice of triumph.

2. FOR THE LORD MOST HIGH IS TER-
-RIBLE; HE IS A GREAT KING OVER
ALL THE EARTH.

3. HE shall subdue the people under us,
and the nations under our feet.

4. HE shall choose our inheritance for
us, the excellency of Jacob
whom HE loved. Selah.

5. GOD is gone up with a shout, the LORD
with the sound of a trumpet

6. SING praises to GOD, sing
praises: sing praises unto
our KING, sing praises.

7. FOR GOD IS THE KING
OF ALL THE EARTH: sing.
ye praises with understanding.

8. **GOD** reigneth over the heathen: sing ye praises with understanding.

9. **The** princes of the people are gathered together, even the people of the **GOD** of **ABRAHAM**: for the shields of the earth belong unto **GOD: HE** is greatly exalted.

PSALM XLVIII.

The ornaments and privileges of the Church.

A Song and Psalm for the sons of Korah.

GREAT IS THE LORD, and greatly to be praised in the city of our **GOD**, in the mountain of **HIS** holiness.

2. **Beautiful** for situation, the joy of the whole earth, is mount **ZION**, on the sides of the north, the city of the great **KING**.

3. GOD IS KNOWN IN HER PALACES FOR A REFUGE.

4. FOR, lo, the kings were assembled, they passed by together.

5. THEY saw it, and so they mar= =velled; they were troubled, and hasted away.

6. FEAR took hold upon them there, and pain, as of a woman in travail.

7. THOU break= =est the ships of TARSHISH with an east wind.

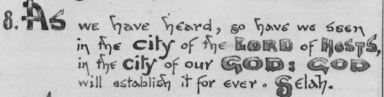

8. AS we have heard, so have we seen in the city of the LORD of HOSTS, in the city of our GOD: GOD will establish it for ever. Selah.

9. WE HAVE THOUGHT OF THY LOVINGKINDNESS, O GOD, IN THE MIDST OF THY TEMPLE.

10. According to thy name, O GOD, so is thy praise unto the ends of the earth: thy right hand is full of righteousness.

11. Let mount ZION rejoice, let the daughters of JUDAH be glad, because of thy judgments.

12. Walk about ZION, and

go round about her: tell the towers thereof.

13. Mark ye well her bul=warks, consider.

·her·palaces;·that·
·ye·may·tell·it·to·the·
·generation·following.·

14.·For·this **GOD** is·our
GOD for·ever·and
ever: **HE** will·be·our
guide·even·unto
death.

PSALM XLIX

1. An earnest persuasion to build the faith of re=
=surrection, not on worldly power, but on
GOD. 16. Worldly prosperity is not to be
admired.

To the chief Musician, A Psalm for the sons
of Korah.

HEAR THIS, all ye people; give ear,
all ye inhabitants of the world:

2. Both low and high, rich and
poor, together.

3. My mouth shall speak of wisdom; and
the meditation of my heart shall be of
understanding.

4. I will incline mine ear to a parable: I will
open my dark saying upon the harp.

5. **Wherefore** should I fear in the days of evil, when the iniquity of my heels shall compass me about?

6. **They** that trust in their wealth, and boast them=selves in the multitude of their riches;

7. **None** of them can by any means redeem his bro=ther, nor give to **GOD** a ransom for him:

8. **For** the redemption of their soul is precious, and it ceaseth for ever:)

9. **That** he should still live for ever, and not see corruption.

10. **For** he seeth that wise men die, likewise the fool and the brutish person perish, and leave their wealth to others.

11. **Their** inward thought is, that their houses shall continue for ever, and their dwelling places to all generations; they call their lands after their own names.

12. **Nevertheless** man being in honour a=bideth not: he is like the beasts that perish.

13. **This** their way is their folly: yet their posterity approve their sayings. Selah.

14. **Like** sheep they are laid in the grave; death shall feed on them; and the up=

=right shall have dominion over them
in the morning; and their beauty shall
consume in the grave from their dwelling.

15. But GOD will redeem my soul from
the power of the grave: for he shall
receive me. Selah.

16. Be not thou afraid when one is made
rich, when the glory of his house
is increased;

17. For when he dieth he shall carry no=
=thing away: his glory shall not
descend after him.

18. Though while he lived he blessed
his soul: and men will praise
thee, when thou doest well to thy=
=self.

19. He shall go to the generation of his
fathers; they shall never see
light.

20. Man that is in honour, and un=
=derstandeth not, is like the
beasts that perish.

PSALM L.

1. The majesty of GOD in the church. 5. HIS order to gather saints. 7. The pleasure of GOD is not in ceremonies, 14. but in sincerity of obedience.

A Psalm of Asaph.

The Mighty even God, the Lord, hath spoken, and called the earth from the rising of the sun unto the going down thereof.

2. Out of Zion, the perfection of beauty, God hath shined.

3. Our God shall come

and shall not keep silence: a fire
shall devour before Him, and it
shall be very tempestous round
about Him.

4. He shall call to the heavens from
above, and to the earth, that He
may judge His people.

5. Gather my saints together unto
me; those that have made a
covenant with me by sacrifice.

6. And the heavens shall
declare His righteousness,
for God is judge Him-
-self. Selah.

7. Hear, O my people, and I
will speak; O Israel,
and I will testify against
thee: I am God, even thy
God.

8 I will not reprove thee for thy sacrifices or thy burnt offerings, to have been continually before Me.

9. I will take no bullock out of thy house, nor he goats out of thy folds.

10. For every beast of the forest is mine, and the cattle upon a thousand hills.

11. I know all the fowls of the moun- -tains: and the wild beasts of the field are mine.

12. If I were hungry, I would not tell thee: for the world is mine, and the fulness thereof.

13. Will I eat the flesh of bulls, or drink the blood of goats?

14. Offer unto God thanksgiving; and pay thy vows unto the most High:

15. And call upon me in the day of trouble: I will deliver thee, and thou shalt glorify me.

16. But unto the wicked God saith, What hast thou to do to declare my statutes, or that thou shouldest take my covenant in thy mouth?

17. Seeing thou hatest instruction, and castest my words behind thee.

18. When thou sawest a thief, then thou consentedst with him, and hast been partaker with adulterers.

19. Thou givest thy mouth to evil, and thy tongue frameth deceit.

20. Thou sittest and speakest against thy brother; thou slanderest thine own mother's son.

21. These things hast thou done, and I kept
silence; thou thoughtest that I was
altogether such an one as thyself: but I
will reprove thee, and set them in order
before thine eyes.

22. Now consider this, ye that forget
GOD, lest I tear you in
pieces, and there be none to deliver.

23. Whoso offereth praise glorifieth me:
and to him that ordereth his con-
=versation aright will I shew the
salvation of GOD.

Psalm LI.

1. David prayeth for remission of
sins, whereof he maketh a deep confession.
6. He prayeth for sanctification. 16. GOD
delighteth not in sacrifice, but in sincerity.
18. He prayeth for the church.

To the chief Musician, A Psalm of David, when Nathan the prophet came unto
him, after he had gone in to Bath-sheba.

HAVE mercy upon me, O God, according to thy lovingkindness: according unto the multitude of thy tender mercies blot out my transgressions. 2. Wash me thoroughly from mine iniquity, and cleanse me from my sin. 3. FOR I ACKNOWLEDGE

MY TRANSGRESSIONS: AND MY SIN IS EVER BEFORE ME.

4. Against THEE, THEE ONLY, HAVE · I · SINNED; AND · DONE · THIS · EVIL · IN · THY · SIGHT: THAT THOU MIGHTEST · BE · JUSTIFIED · WHEN · THOU SPEAKEST, AND · BE · CLEAR · WHEN THOU ·JUDGEST.

5. Behold, I was shapen in iniquity: and in sin did my mother conceive me.

6. Behold, THOU desirest truth in the inward parts: and in the hidden *part* THOU shalt make me to know wisdom.

7. PURGE ME WITH HYSSOP, AND I. SHALL BE CLEAN: WASH ME, AND I. SHALL BE WHITER THAN SNOW

8. Make me to hear joy and glad-ness; THAT the bones WHICH THOU hast broken may rejoice.

9. HIDE · THY · FACE · FROM · MY · SINS, AND · BLOT · OUT · ALL · MINE · INIQUITIES:

10. CREATE·IN·ME·A·CLEAN·HEART; ·O·GOD·; AND·RENEW·A· RIGHT·SPIRIT·WITHIN·ME:

11. Cast me not away from thy pre= =sence; and take not thy holy spirit from me.

12. Restore unto me the joy of thy salvation; and uphold me with thy free spirit.

13. THEN WILL I TEACH TRANSGRESSORS THY WAYS; AND SINNERS SHALL BE CONVERT= =ED UNTO THEE.

14. Deliver me from blood-guiltiness, O GOD, thou God of my salvation: and my tongue shall sing aloud of thy right= =eousness.

15. O LORD, OPEN THOU MY LIPS; AND MY MOUTH SHALL SHEW FORTH THY PRAISE.

16. For thou desireth not sacrifice; else would I give it: thou delightest not in burnt- offering.

17. The sacrifices of God are a broken spirit: a broken and a contrite heart, O GOD, thou wilt not despise.

18. Do good in thy good pleasure unto ZION: build thou the walls of JERUSALEM.

19. Then shalt thou be pleased with the sacrifices of righteousness, with burnt offering and whole burnt offering: then shall they offer bullocks upon thine altar.

PSALM ✠ LII.

1. David, condemning the spitefulness of Doeg, prophesieth his destruction. 6. The righteous shall rejoice at it. 8. David, upon his confidence in **GOD**'s mercy, giveth thanks.

To the chief Musician, Maschil, A Psalm of David, when Doeg the Edomite came and told Saul, and said unto him, David is come to the house of Ahimelech.

WHY boastest thou thyself in mischief, O mighty man? the goodness of **GOD** endureth continually.

2. Thy tongue deviseth mischiefs;

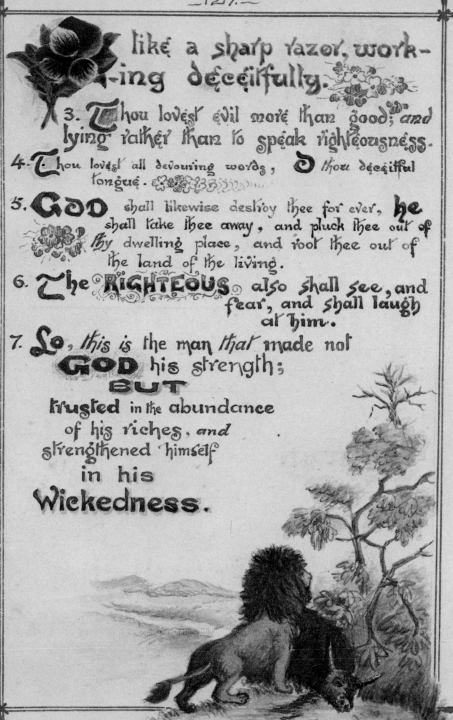

like a sharp razor, work-ing deceitfully.

3. Thou lovest evil more than good; and lying rather than to speak righteousness.

4. Thou lovest all devouring words, O thou deceitful tongue.

5. GOD shall likewise destroy thee for ever, he shall take thee away, and pluck thee out of thy dwelling place, and root thee out of the land of the living.

6. The RIGHTEOUS also shall see, and fear, and shall laugh at him.

7. Lo, this is the man that made not GOD his strength; BUT trusted in the abundance of his riches, and strengthened himself in his Wickedness.

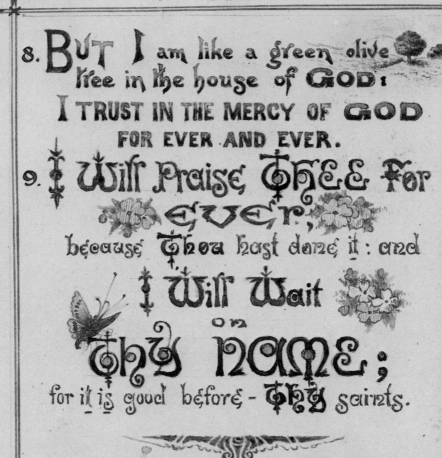

8. BUT I am like a green olive tree in the house of GOD: I TRUST IN THE MERCY OF GOD FOR EVER AND EVER.

9. I Will Praise THEE For EVER, because Thou hast done it: and I Will Wait on THY NAME; for it is good before - THY saints.

PSALM · LIII. ·

1. David describeth the corruption of a natural man. 4. He convinceth the wicked by the light of their own wicked conscience. 6. He glorieth in the salvation of GOD. To the chief Musician upon Mahalath, Maschil, A Psalm of David.

1. **T**he fool hath said in his heart, there is no **GOD.** Corrupt are they, and have done abominable iniquity: *there is* none that doeth good.

2. **GOD** looked down from **heaven** upon the children of men, to see if there were any that did understand, that did seek **GOD.**

3. Every one of them is gone back: they are altogether become filthy; there is none that doeth good, no, not one.

4. Have the workers of iniquity no know-ledge? who eat up my people as they eat bread: they have not call-ed upon GOD.

5. There were they in great fear, where no fear was: for GOD hath scat-tered the bones of him that encamp-eth against thee: thou hast put them to shame, because GOD hath des-pised them.

6. Oh that the salvation of ISRAEL were come out of ZION! When GOD bringeth back the captivity of his people, JACOB shall rejoice, and ISRAEL shall be glad.

131.

PSALM LIV.

¶ 1. David, complaining of the Ziphims, prayeth for sal=vation. 4. Upon his confidence in **GOD'S** help he promiseth sacrifice.

To the chief Mus=ician on Neginoth, Maschil. A Psalm of David, when the Ziphims came and said to Saul, Doth not Da=vid hide himself with us?

1. SAVE me, O God, by thy name, and judge me by thy strength.

2. Hear my prayer, O God; give ear to the words of my mouth.

3 FOR strangers are risen up against me, and oppressors seek after my soul: they have not set GOD before them. Selah.

4. BEHOLD, GOD IS MINE HELPER: THE LORD IS WITH THEM THAT UPHOLD MY SOUL.

5. **HE** shall reward evil unto mine enemies: cut them off in **thy** truth.

6. **I** will freely sacrifice unto **thee**: **I WILL PRAISE THY NAME, O LORD**; for *it is* good.

7. **FOR HE** hath delivered me out of all trouble: and mine eye hath seen *his desire* upon mine enemies.

PSALM LV.

1. *David in his prayer complaineth of his fearful case.* 9. *He prayeth against his enemies, of whose wick=edness and treachery he complain=eth.* 16. *He comforteth himself in* GOD'S *preservation of him, and confusion of his enemies.*

To the chief Musician on Neginoth, Maschil, A Psalm of David.

GIVE·EAR·TO·MY·PRAYER O·GOD; AND·HIDE·NOT·THY -SELF·FROM·MY·SUPPLICA--TION.

2. Attend unto me, and hear me: I mourn in my complaint, and make a noise;

3. Because of the voice of the enemy, because of the oppression of the wicked: for they cast iniquity upon me, and in wrath they hate me.

4. My heart is sore pained within me: and the terrors of death are fallen upon me.

5. Fearfulness and trembling are come upon me, and horror hath overwhelmed me.

6. And I said, OH THAT I HAD WINGS LIKE A DOVE! FOR THEN WOULD I FLY AWAY, AND BE AT REST.

7. Lo, then would I wander far off, and remain in the wilderness. Selah.

8. I would hasten my escape from the windy storm and tempest.

9. Destroy, O LORD, and divide their tongues: for I have seen violence and strife in the city.

10. Day and night they go about it upon the walls thereof: mischief also and sorrow are in the midst of it.

11. Wickedness is in the midst thereof: deceit and guile depart not from her streets.

12. For it was not an enemy that reproached me; then I could have borne it: neither was it he that hated me that did magnify himself against me; then I would have hid myself from him:

13. But it was thou, a man mine equal, my guide, and mine acquaintance.

14. We took sweet counsel together, and walked into the house of GOD in company.

15. Let death seize upon them, and let them go down quick into hell: for wickedness is in their dwellings and among them.

16. As for me, I WILL CALL UPON GOD; AND THE LORD SHALL SAVE ME.

17. Evening, and morning, and at noon, will I pray, and cry aloud: and he shall hear my voice.

18. He hath delivered my soul in peace from the battle that was against me: for there were many with me

19. **GOD** shall hear, and afflict them, even he that abideth of old. Selah. Because they have no changes, therefore they fear not **GOD**.

20. **H**e hath put forth his hands against such as be at peace with him: he hath broken his covenant.

21. **T**he words of his mouth were smoother than butter, but war was in his heart: his words were softer than oil, yet were they drawn swords.

22. **CAST THY BURDEN UPON THE LORD, AND HE SHALL SUSTAIN THEE: HE SHALL NEVER SUFFER THE RIGHT= =EOUS TO BE MOVED.**

23. **B**ut thou, **O GOD**, shalt bring them down into the pit of destruction: bloody and deceitful men shall not live out half their days; but _____

I will trust in thee.

PSALM LVI.

1. David, praying to GOD in con=
=fidence of his word, complain=
=eth of his enemies. 9. Hee profess=
=eth his confidence in God's word,
and promiseth to praise him.

To the chief Musician upon Jonath-elem-rechokim, Michtam of
David when the Philistines took him in Gath.

1. Be merciful unto me, O GOD:
for man would swallow me up; he fighting daily
oppresseth me.
2. Mine enemies would daily swallow me up: for
they be many that fight against me, O
O thou most High.
3. What time I am afraid, I will trust in
thee.
4. In GOD I will praise his word, in GOD I
have put my trust; I will not fear what
flesh can do unto me.
5. Every day they wrest my words: all their
thoughts are against me for evil.
6. They gather themselves together, they hide them-
-selves, they mark my steps, when
they wait for my soul.
7. Shall they escape by iniquity? in
thine anger cast down the
people, O GOD.
8. Thou tellest my wanderings:
put thou my tears into
thy bottle: are they
not in thy book?

9. WHEN I cry unto thee, then shall mine enemies turn back: this I know; for GOD IS FOR ME.

10. In GOD will I praise his word: in the LORD will I praise his word.

11. In GOD have I put my trust: I will not be afraid what man can do unto me.

12. Thy vows are upon me, O GOD: I will render praises unto thee.

13. For thou hast delivered my soul from death: wilt not thou deliver my feet from falling, that I may walk before GOD in the light of the living?

PSALM LVII.

1. David in prayer fleeing unto GOD complaineth of his dangerous case.
7. He encourageth himself to praise GOD.

To the chief Musician, Al-taschith, Michtam of David,— when he fled from Saul in the cave.

BE merciful unto me, O GOD, be merciful unto me: for my soul trusteth in thee: yea, in the shadow of thy wings will I make my refuge, until these calamities be overpast.

2. I will cry unto **GOD** most high; unto **GOD** that performeth all things for me.

3. **He** shall send from heaven, and save me from the reproach of him that would swallow me up. Selah. **GOD** shall send forth his mercy and his truth.

4. **My** soul is among lions: and I lie even among them that are set on fire, even the sons of men, whose teeth are spears and arrows, and their tongue a sharp sword.

5. BE THOU EXALTED O GOD ABOVE THE HEAVENS; LET THY GLORY BE ABOVE ALL THE EARTH.

6. They have prepared a net for my steps; my soul is bowed down: they have dig-
-ged a pit before me, into the midst where-
-of they are fallen themselves. Selah.

7. MY HEART IS FIXED, O GOD, MY HEART IS FIXED: I WILL SING AND GIVE PRAISE.

8. AWAKE UP, MY GLORY; AWAKE, PSALTERY AND HARP: I MYSELF WILL AWAKE-
-EARLY.

9. I will praise thee, O LORD, among the people: I will sing unto thee among the nations.

10. For thy mercy is great unto the heavens, and thy truth unto the clouds.

11. Be thou exalted, O GOD, above the heavens: let thy glory be above all the earth.

PSALM LVIII.

1. David reproveth wicked judges,
3. describeth the nature of the wicked,
6. devoteth them to God's judgments,
10. whereat the righteous shall rejoice.

To the chief Musician, Al-taschith, Michtam of David.

Do ye indeed speak righteousness, O con-gregation? do ye judge uprightly, O ye sons of men?

2. Yea, in heart ye work wickedness; ye weigh the violence of your hands in the earth.

3. The wicked are estranged from the womb: they go astray as soon as they be born, speaking lies.

4. Their poison is like the poison of a serpent: they are like the deaf adder that stoppeth her ear.

5. Which will not hearken to the voice of charmers, charming never so wisely.

6. Break their teeth, O GOD, in their mouth: break out the great teeth of the young lions, O LORD.

7. Let them melt away as waters which run continually: when he bendeth his bow to shoot his arrows, let them be as cut in pieces.

8. As a snail which melteth, let every one of them pass away: like the untimely birth of a woman, that they may not see the sun.

9. Before your pots can feel the thorns, he shall take them away as with a whirlwind, both living, and in his wrath.

10. The righteous shall rejoice when he seeth the ven-geance: he shall wash his feet in the blood of the wicked.

11. So that a man shall say, Verily there is a re-ward for the righteous: verily he is a GOD that judgeth in the earth.

PSALM LIX.

1. *David prayeth to be delivered from his enemies.* 6. *He complaineth of their cruelty.*
8. *He trusteth in God.* 11. *He prayeth against them.* 16. *He praiseth God.*
To the chief Musician, Al-taschith, Michtam of David; when Saul sent, and
they watched the house to kill him.

DELIVER me from mine enemies, O my GOD: defend me
from them that rise up against me.

2. Deliver me from the workers of iniquity, and save me
from bloody men.

3. For, lo, they lie in wait for my soul: the mighty are gather-
-ed against me; not for my transgression, nor for
my sin, O LORD.

4. They run and prepare themselves without my fault: awake
to help me, and behold.

5. THOU therefore, O LORD GOD of hosts, the GOD of
Israel, awake to visit all the heathen: be not merciful
to any wicked transgressors. Selah.

6. They return at evening: they make a noise like a dog, and go
round about the city.

7. Behold, they belch out with their mouth: swords are in their
lips: for who, say they, doth hear?

8. But thou, O LORD, shalt laugh at
them; thou shalt have all the
heathen in derision.

TEMPLE OF VESTA AT TIVOLI NEAR ROME.

9. Because of his strength will I wait upon thee : for

GOD IS MY DEFENCE.

10. The **GOD** of my mercy shall prevent me: **GOD** shall let me see my desire upon mine enemies.

11. Slay them not, lest my people forget: scatter them by thy power; and bring them down, **O LORD** our shield.

12. For the sin of their mouth and the words of their lips let them even be taken in their pride: and for cursing and lying which they speak.

13. Consume them in wrath, consume them, that they may not be: and let them know that **GOD** ruleth in Jacob unto the ends of the earth. Selah.

14. And at evening let them return; and let them make a noise like a dog, and go round about the city.

15. Let them wander up and down for meat, and grudge if they be not satisfied.

16. But I will sing of thy power; yea I will sing aloud of thy mercy in the morning : for thou hast been my defence and refuge in the day of my trouble.

17. Unto thee, O my strength, will I sing: for God is my defence, and the God of my refuge.

PSALM LX.

1. David, complaining to God of former judgment, 4 now, upon better hope, prayeth for deliverance. 6 Comforting himself in God's promises, he craveth that help whereon he trusteth.

To the chief Musician upon Shushaneduth, Michtam of David, to teach; when he strove with Aram-naharaim and with Aram-zobah, when Joab returned, and smote of Edom in the valley of salt twelve thousand.

O GOD, thou hast cast us off, thou hast scattered us, thou hast been displeased; O turn thyself to us again.

2. Thou hast made the earth to tremble; thou hast broken it: heal the breaches thereof; for it shaketh.

3. Thou hast showed thy people hard things: thou hast made us to drink the wine of astonishment.

4. Thou hast given a banner to them that fear thee, that it may be displayed because of the truth. Selah.

5. That thy beloved may be delivered; save with thy right hand, and hear me.

6. GOD hath spoken in his holiness; I will rejoice, I will divide Shechem, and mete out the valley of Succoth.

7. Gilead is mine, and Manasseh is mine; Ephraim also is the strength of mine head; Judah is my lawgiver;

8. Moab is my washpot; over Edom will I cast out my shoe: Philistia, triumph thou because of me.

9. Who will bring me into the strong city? who will lead me into Edom?

10. Wilt not thou, O GOD, which hadst cast us off? and thou, O GOD, which didst not go out with our armies?

11. **GIVE US HELP FROM TROUBLE:**
FOR VAIN IS THE HELP OF MAN.

12. THROUGH GOD WE SHALL DO VALIANT-
-LY: FOR HE IT IS THAT SHALL
TREAD DOWN OUR ENEMIES.

PSALM LXI.

1. *David fleeth to God upon his former experience. 4. He voweth perpetual service unto Him, because of his promises.*
To the chief Musician upon Neginah. A Psalm of David.

HEAR my cry, O GOD; attend
unto my prayer.

2. From the end of the earth will I cry unto thee,
   when my heart is overwhelmed: lead me
   to the rock that is higher than I.

3. For thou hast been a shelter for me, and a strong
   tower from the enemy.

4. I will abide in thy tabernacle for ever: I will
   trust in the covert of thy wings. Selah.

5. For thou, O GOD, hast heard my vows:
   thou hast given me the heritage of
   those that fear thy name.

6. **Thou** wilt prolong the
king's life:
and his years as many
generations.

7. **He** shall abide before
GOD for ever: O
prepare mercy and
truth, which may preserve him

8. **So** will I sing praise unto
thy name for ever,
that I may daily
perform my vows.

PSALM LXII.

1. David professing his confidence in GOD dis=
courageth his enemies. 5. In the same confidence he
encourageth the godly. 9. No trust is to be put in
worldly things. 11. Power and mercy belong to GOD.
To the chief Musician, to Jeduthun, A Psalm of David.

TRULY MY SOUL WAITETH UPON
GOD: FROM HIM COMETH MY SAL-
-VATION.

2. HE ONLY IS MY ROCK AND MY SALVATION; HE IS MY DEFENCE; I SHALL NOT BE GREATLY MOVED.

3. HOW long will ye imagine mischief against a man? ye shall be slain all of you: as a bowing wall shall ye be, and as a tottering fence.

4. THEY only consult to cast him down from his excellency: they delight in lies: they bless with their mouth, but they curse inwardly. Selah.

5. MY SOUL, WAIT THOU ONLY UPON GOD; FOR MY EXPECTATION IS FROM HIM.

6. HE ONLY IS MY ROCK AND MY SALVATION: HE IS MY DEFENCE; I SHALL NOT BE MOVED.

7. IN GOD IS MY SALVATION AND MY GLORY: THE ROCK OF MY STRENGTH, AND MY REFUGE, IS IN GOD.

8. TRUST IN HIM AT ALL TIMES; ye people, POUR OUT YOUR HEART BEFORE HIM: GOD IS A REFUGE FOR US. Selah.

9. SURELY men of low degree are vanity, and men of high degree are a lie: to be laid in the balance, they are altogether lighter than vanity.

10. TRUST not in oppression, and become not vain in robbery: if riches increase, set not your heart upon them.

11. GOD hath spoken once; twice have I heard this; that —

POWER BELONGETH UNTO GOD.

12. ALSO UNTO THEE, O LORD, BE= =LONGETH MERCY, for thou renderest to every man according to his work.

PSALM LXIII.

1. Davids thirst for God.
2. His manner of blessing God.
9. His confidence of his enemies' destruction, and his own safety.

A Psalm of David, when he was in the wilderness — of Judah.

O GOD, thou <u>art</u> my GOD; early will I seek thee: my soul thirsteth for thee, my flesh longeth for thee in a dry and thirsty land, where no water is;

2. To see thy power and thy glory, so <u>as</u> I have seen thee in the sanctuary.

3. Because thy loving-kindness is better than life, my lips shall praise thee.

4. Thus will I bless thee while I live: I will lift up my hands in thy name.

5. My soul shall be satisfied as <u>with</u> marrow and fatness; and my mouth shall praise <u>thee</u> with joyful lips:

6. When I remember thee upon my bed, and meditate on thee in the night watches.

7. Because thou hast been my help, therefore in the sha=dow of thy wings will I rejoice.

8. My soul followeth hard after thee: thy right hand up-holdeth me.

9. But those that seek my soul, to destroy it, shall go into the lower parts of the earth.

10. They shall fall by the sword: they shall be a portion for foxes.

11. But the king shall rejoice in GOD; every one that sweareth by him shall glory: but the mouth of them that speak lies shall be stopped.

PSALM LXIV.

1. David prayeth for deliverance, complaining of his enemies. 7. He promiseth him-self to see such an evident destruction of his enemies, as the righteous shall rejoice at it.

To the chief Musician, A Psalm of David.

Hear my voice, O GOD, in my prayer: preserve my life from fear of the enemy.

2. Hide me from the secret counsel of the wicked; from the insurrection of the workers of iniquity.

3. Who whet their tongue like a sword, <u>and</u> bend <u>their bows to shoot</u> their arrows, <u>even</u> bitter words.

4. That they may shoot in secret at the perfect: suddenly do they shoot at him, and fear not.

5. They encourage themselves in an evil matter: they com-mune of laying snares privily; they say, Who shall see them?

6. They search out iniquities; they accomplish a diligent search: both the inward thought of every one of them, and the heart, is deep.

7. But GOD shall shoot at them with an arrow; suddenly shall they be wounded.

8. So they shall make their own tongue to fall upon them=selves: all that see them shall flee away.

9. And all men shall fear, and shall declare the work of GOD; for they shall wisely consider of his doing.

10. The righteous shall be glad in the LORD, and shall trust in him; and all the upright in heart shall glory.

PSALM LXV.

1. David praiseth God for his grace. 4. The blessedness of God's chosen by reason of benefits.

To the chief Musician, A Psalm and Song of David

1. Praise waiteth for thee, O GOD, in Sion: and unto thee shall the vow be performed.

2. O thou that hearest prayer, unto thee shall all flesh come.

3. Iniquities prevail against me: as for our transgress=ions, thou shalt purge them away.

4. Blessed is the man whom thou choosest, and causeth to approach unto thee, that he may dwell in thy courts: we shall be satisfied with the goodness of thy house, even of thy holy temple.

5. By terrible things in righteousness wilt thou answer us, O GOD of our salvation; who art the confid=ence of all the ends of the earth, and of them that are afar off upon the sea:

6. Which by his strength setteth fast the mountains; being girded with power:

7. Which stilleth the noise of the seas, the noise of their waves, and the tumult of the people.

8. They also that dwell in the uttermost parts are afraid at thy tokens: thou makest the outgoings of the morning and evening to rejoice.

9. Thou visitest the earth, and waterest it: thou greatly enrichest it with the river of GOD, which is full of water: thou preparest them corn, when thou hast so provided for it.

10. Thou waterest the ridges thereof abundantly: thou settlest the furrows thereof: thou makest it soft with showers: thou blessest the springing thereof.

11. Thou crownest the year with thy goodness; and thy paths drop fatness.

12. They drop upon the pastures of the wilderness: and the little hills rejoice on every side.

13. The pastures are clothed with flocks; the valleys also are covered over with corn; they shout for joy, they also sing.

PSALM LXVI.

1. David exhorteth to praise GOD, 5. to observe his great works, 8 to bless him for his gracious benefits. 12. He voweth for himself religious service to GOD. 16. He declareth GOD's special goodness to himself.

To the chief Musician, A Song or Psalm.

MAKE a joyful noise unto GOD, all ye lands:

2. Sing forth the honour of his name: make his praise glorious.

3. Say unto GOD, How terrible art thou in thy works! through the greatness of thy power shall thine enemies submit themselves unto thee.

4. All the earth shall worship thee, and shall sing unto thee; they shall sing to thy name. Selah.

5. Come and see the works of GOD: he is terrible in his doing toward the children of men.

6. He turned the sea into dry land: they went through the flood on foot: there did we rejoice in him.

7. He ruleth by his power for ever; his eyes behold the nations: let not the rebellious exalt themselves. Selah.

8. O bless our GOD, ye people, and make the voice of his praise to be heard:

9. Which holdeth our soul in life, and suffereth not our feet to be moved.

10. For thou, O GOD, hast proved us: thou hast tried us, as silver is tried.

11. Thou broughtest us into the net; thou laidst affliction upon our loins.

12. Thou hast caused men to ride over our heads; we went through fire and through water: but thou broughtest us out into a wealthy place.

13. I will go into thy house with burnt offerings: I will pay thee my vows,

14. Which my lips have uttered, and my mouth hath spoken, when I was in trouble.

15. I will offer unto thee burnt sacrifices of fatlings, with the incense of rams; I will offer bullocks with goats. Selah.

16. Come and hear, all ye that fear GOD, and I will declare what he hath done for my soul.

17. I cried unto him with my mouth, and he was extolled with my tongue.

18. If I regard iniquity in my heart, the **LORD** will not hear <u>me</u>:

19. But verily **GOD** hath heard <u>me</u>; he hath attended to the voice of my prayer.

20. Blessed be **GOD**, which hath not turned away my prayer, nor his mercy from me.

PSALM LXVII.

1. A prayer for the enlargement of GOD'S kingdom, 3. to the joy of the people, 6. and the increase of — GOD'S blessings.

To the chief Musician on Neginoth, A Psalm or Song.

God be merciful unto us, and bless us; and cause his face to shine upon us; Selah.

2. That thy way may be known upon earth, thy saving health among all nations.

3. Let the people praise thee, O God;
let all the people praise thee.

4. O let the nations be glad and sing
for joy: for thou shalt judge the
people righteously, and
govern the nations
upon earth. Selah.

5. Let the people praise thee,
O God; let all the peo-
ple praise thee.

6. Then shall the
earth yield her increase;
and God, even our
own God, shall bless
us.

7. God shall bless us;
and all the ends
of the earth shall
fear him.

PSALM LXVIII.

1. A prayer at the removing of the ark.
4. An exhortation to praise GOD for his mercies, 7. for his care of the church, 19. for his great works.

To the chief Musician, A Psalm or Song of David.

LET GOD arise, let his enemies be scattered: let them also that hate him flee before him.

2. As smoke is driven away, so drive them away: as wax melteth before the fire, so let the wicked perish at the presence of GOD.

3. But let the righteous be glad; let them rejoice before GOD: yea, let them exceedingly re=joice.

4. Sing unto GOD, sing praises to his name: extol him that rideth upon the heavens by his name JAH, and rejoice before him.

5. A father of the fatherless, and a judge of the widows, is GOD in his holy habitation.

6. GOD setteth the solitary in families: he bringeth out those which are bound with chains: but the rebellious dwell in a dry land.

7. O GOD, when thou wentest forth before thy people, when thou didst march through the wilderness; Selah:

8. The earth shook, the heavens also dropped at the presence of GOD: even Sinai was=moved at the presence of GOD=, the GOD of Israel.

9. Thou, O GOD, didst send a plentiful rain, whereby thou didst confirm thine inheritance, when it was weary.

10. THY congregation hath dwelt therein: thou, O GOD, hast prepared of thy goodness for the poor.

11. The LORD gave the word: great was the company of those that published it.

12. Kings of armies did flee apace: and she that tarried at home divided the spoil.

13. Though ye have lien among the pots, yet shall ye be as the wings of a dove covered with silver, and her feathers with yellow gold.

14. When the ALMIGHTY scattered kings in it, it was white as snow in Salmon.

15. The hill of GOD is as the hill of Bashan; an high hill as the hill of Bashan.

16. Why leap ye, ye hills? this is the hill which GOD desireth to dwell in; yea, the LORD will dwell in it for ever.

17. The chariots of GOD are twenty thousand, even thousands of angels: the LORD is among them, as in SINAI, in the holy place.

18. Thou hast ascended on high, thou hast led captivity captive: thou hast received gifts for men; yea, for the rebellious also, that the LORD GOD might dwell among them.

19. Blessed be the LORD, who daily loadeth us with benefits, even the GOD of our salvation. Selah.

20. HE that is our **GOD** is the **GOD** of salvation; and unto **GOD** the **LORD** belong the issues from death.

21. But **GOD** shall wound the head of his enemies, and the hairy scalp of such an one as goeth on still in his trespasses.

22. The LORD said, I will bring again from **Bashan**, I will bring my people again from the depths of the sea:

23. That thy foot may be dipped in the blood of thine enemies, and the tongue of thy dogs in the same.

24. They have seen thy goings, **O GOD**; even the goings of my **GOD**, my **KING**, in the sanctuary.

25. The singers went before, the players on in= =struments followed after; among them- -were the damsels playing with timbrels.

26. Bless ye **GOD** in the congregations, even the **LORD**, from the fountain of **Israel**.

27. There is little **Benjamin** with their ruler, the princes of **Judah** and their council, the princes of **Zebulun**, and the princes of **Naphtali**.

28. Thy **GOD** hath commanded thy strength: strengthen, **O GOD**, that which thou hast wrought for us.

29. Because of thy temple at Jer- =usalem shall kings bring presents unto thee.

30. Rebuke the company of spearmen, the multitude of the bulls, with the calves of the people, <u>till every one</u> submit himself with pieces of silver: scatter thou the people that delight in war.

31. Princes shall come out of Egypt; Ethiopia shall soon stretch out her hands unto GOD.

32. Sing unto GOD, ye kingdoms of the earth; O sing praises unto the LORD; Selah.

33. To him that rideth upon the heavens of heavens, <u>which were</u> of old; lo, he doth send out his voice, <u>and that</u> a mighty voice.

34. Ascribe ye strength unto GOD: his excellency <u>is</u> over Israel, and his strength <u>is</u> in the clouds.

35 O GOD, thou art terrible out of thy holy places: the GOD of Israel <u>is</u> he that giveth strength and power unto <u>his</u> people. Blessed <u>be</u> GOD.

PSALM LXIX.

1. David complain= zeth of his affliction. 13. He prayeth for de= liverance. 22. He devoteth his enemies to destruction. 30. He praiseth God with thanksgiving.

To the chief Musician upon Shoshan= =nim. A Psalm of David.

SAVE me, O GOD; for the waters are come in unto my soul.

2. I sink in deep mire, where there is no standing: I am come into deep waters, where the floods overflow me.

3. I am weary of my crying: my throat is dried: mine eyes fail while I wait for my GOD

4. They that hate me without a cause are more than the hairs of mine head: they that would de= stroy me, being mine enemies wrongfully, are mighty: then I restored that which I took not away.

5. O GOD, thou knowest my foolishness; and my sins are not hid from thee.

6. Let not them that wait on thee, O LORD GOD of hosts, be ashamed for my sake: let not those that seek thee be confounded for my sake, O GOD of ISRAEL.

7. Because for thy sake I have borne reproach; shame hath covered my face.

8. I am become a stranger unto my brethren, and an alien unto my mother's children.

9. For the zeal of thine house hath eaten me up; and the reproaches of them that reproached thee are fallen upon me.

10. When I wept, and chastened my soul with fasting, that was to my reproach.

11. I made sackcloth also my garment; and became a proverb to them.

12. They that sit in the gate speak against me; and I was the song of the drunkards.

13. But as for me, my prayer is unto thee, O LORD, in an acceptable time: O GOD, in the multitude of thy mercy hear me, in the truth of thy sal=vation.

14. Deliver me out of the mire, and let me not sink: let me be delivered from them that hate me, and out of the deep waters.

15. Let not the waterflood overflow me, neither let the deep swallow me up, and let not the pit shut her mouth upon me.

16. **Hear me, O LORD**; for thy lovingkindness is good: turn unto me according to the multitude of thy tender mercies.

17. **And** hide not thy face from thy servant; for I am in trouble: hear me speedily.

18. **Draw** nigh unto my soul, and redeem it: deliver me because of mine enemies.

19. **Thou** hast known my reproach, and my shame, and my dishonour: mine adversaries are all before thee.

20. **Reproach** hath broken my heart; and I am full of heaviness: and I looked for some to take pity, but there was none; and for comforters, but I found none.

21. **They** gave me also gall for my meat; and in my thirst they gave me vinegar to drink.

22. **Let** their table become a snare before them: and that which should have been for their welfare, let it become a trap.

23. **Let** their eyes be darkened, that they see not; and make their loins continually to shake.

24. **Pour** out thine indignation upon them, and let thy wrathful anger take hold of them.

25. **Let** their habitation be desolate; and let none dwell in their tents.

26. **For** they persecute him whom thou hast smitten; and they talk to the grief of those whom thou hast wounded.

27. **Add** iniquity unto their iniquity: and let them not come into thy righteousness.

28. **Let** them be blotted out of the book of the living, and not be written with the righteous.

29. But I am poor and sorrowful; let thy salvation, O GOD, set me up on high.

30. I will praise the name of GOD with a song, and will magnify him with thanksgiving.

31. This also shall please the LORD better than an ox or bullock that hath horns and hoofs.

32. The humble shall see this, and be glad: and your heart shall live that seek GOD.

33. FOR · THE · LORD · HEARETH · THE · POOR, AND · DESPISETH · NOT · HIS · PRISONERS.

34. Let the heaven and earth praise him, the seas, and every thing that moveth therein.

35. For GOD will save Zion, and will build the cities of Judah: that they may dwell there, and have it in possession.

36. The seed also of his servants shall inherit it: and they that love his name shall dwell therein.

Psalm LXX

David soliciteth GOD to the speedy destruction of the wicked, and preservation of the godly.

To the chief Musician, A Psalm of David, to bring to remembrance.

MAKE haste, O. GOD, to deliver me, make haste to help me, O LORD.

2. Let them be ashamed and confounded that seek af=
:ter my soul: let them be turned backward,
and put to confusion, that desire my hurt.

3. Let them be turned back for a reward of their
shame that say, Aha, aha.

4. Let all those that seek thee rejoice and be
glad in thee: and let such as love thy
salvation say continually, **LET GOD BE
MAGNIFIED.**

5. But I am poor and needy: make haste unto
ME, O GOD: thou art my help and
my deliverer; O LORD, make no
tarrying.

Psalm LXXI

1. *David, in confidence of faith, and experience of God's fa=
=vour, prayeth both for himself, and against the enemies of his
soul. 14. He promiseth constancy. 17. He prayeth for perser=
=erance. 19. He praiseth God, and promiseth to do it cheer=
=fully*

IN THEE, O LORD, DO I PUT MY
TRUST: LET ME NEVER BE PUT TO
CONFUSION.

2. **Deliver** me in thy righteousness, and cause me to escape:
incline thine ear unto me, and save me.

3. **Be** thou my strong habitation, whereunto I may contin=
=ually resort: thou hast given commandment to save
me; for **thou art my rock and my fortress.**

4. **Deliver** me, O my GOD, out of the hand of the
wicked, out of the hand of the unrighteous and
cruel man.

5. For thou art my hope, O Lord God: thou art my trust from my youth.

6. By thee have I been holden up from the womb: thou art he that took me out of my mother's bowels: my praise shall be continually of thee.

7. I am as a wonder unto many; but thou art my strong refuge.

8. Let my mouth be filled with thy praise and with thy honour all the day.

9. Cast me not off in the time of old age; forsake me not when my strength faileth.

10. For mine enemies speak against me; and they that lay wait for my soul take counsel together.

11. Saying, God hath forsaken him: persecute and take him; for there is none to deliver him.

12. O God, be not far from me: O my God, make haste for my help.

13. Let them be confounded and consumed that are adver=saries to my soul; let them be covered with re=proach and dishonour that seek my hurt.

14. But I will hope continually, and will yet praise thee more and more.

15. My mouth shall shew forth thy righteous=ness and thy salvation all the day; for I know not the numbers thereof.

16. I will go in the strength of the Lord God: I will make mention of thy righteousness, even of thine only.

17. O God, thou hast taught me from my youth: and hitherto have I declared thy wondrous works.

18. **Now** also when I am old and greyheaded, **O GOD**, forsake me not; until I have shewed thy strength unto this generation, and thy power to every one that is to come.

19. **Thy** righteousness also, **O GOD**, is very high, who hath done these things: **O GOD**, who is like unto thee!

20. **Thou**, which hast shewed me great and sore troubles, shall quicken me again, and shalt bring me up again from the depths of the earth.

21. **Thou** shalt increase my greatness, and comfort me on every side.

22. **I WILL ALSO PRAISE THEE WITH THE PSALTERY, EVEN THY TRUTH, O MY GOD: UNTO THEE WILL I SING WITH THE HARP, O THOU HOLY ONE OF ISRAEL.**

23. **My** lips shall greatly rejoice when I sing unto thee; and my soul, which thou hast redeemed.

24. **My** tongue also shall talk of thy righteousness all the day long: for they are confounded, for they are brought unto shame, that seek my hurt.

PSALM LXXII.

1. *David, praying for Solomon, sheweth the goodness and glory of his, in type, and in truth, of* Christ's kingdom. 18. *He blesseth* GOD.

A Psalm for Solomon.

Give the king thy judgments, **O GOD**, and thy righteousness unto the king's son.

2. HE shall judge thy people with righteousness, and thy poor with judgment.

3. THE mountains shall bring peace to the people, and the little hills, by righteousness.

4. HE shall judge the poor of the people, he shall save the children of the needy, and shall break in pieces the oppressor.

5. THEY shall fear thee as long as the sun and moon endure, throughout all generations.

6. HE shall come down like rain upon the mown grass: as showers that water the earth.

7. IN his days shall the righteous flourish; and abundance of peace so long as the moon endureth.

8. HE shall have dominion also from sea to sea, and from the river unto the ends of the earth.

9. THEY that dwell in the wilderness shall bow before him; and his enemies shall lick the dust.

10. THE kings of Tarshish and of the isles shall bring presents: the kings of Sheba and Seba shall offer gifts.

11. YEA, all kings shall fall down before him: all nations shall serve him.

12. FOR he shall deliver the needy when he crieth; the poor also, and him that hath no helper.

13. HE shall spare the poor and needy, and shall save the souls of the needy.

14. HE shall redeem their soul from deceit and violence: and precious shall their blood be in his sight.

15. AND he shall live, and to him shall be given of the gold of Sheba: prayer also shall be made for him continually; and daily shall he be praised.

16. THERE shall be an handful of corn in the earth upon the top of the mountains; the fruit thereof shall shake like Lebanon: and they of the city shall flourish like grass of the earth.

17. HIS name shall endure for ever: his name shall be continued as long as the sun: and men shall be blessed in him: all nations shall call him blessed.

18. Blessed be the LORD GOD, the GOD of ISRAEL, who only doeth wondrous things.

19. AND blessed be his glorious name for ever: and let the whole earth be filled with his glory; Amen, and Amen.

20. THE prayers of David the son of JESSE are ended.

PSALM ✻ LXXIII.

A Psalm of Asaph.

TRULY GOD is good to Israel, even to such
as are of a clean heart.

2. But as for me, my feet were almost gone; my
steps had well nigh slipped.

3. For I was envious at the foolish, when I saw
the prosperity of the wicked.

4. For there are no bands in their death: but
their strength is firm.

5. They are not in trouble as other men; neither
are they plagued like other men.

6. Therefore pride compasseth them about as a
chain; violence covereth them as a gar-
-ment.

7. Their eyes stand out with fatness: they have
more than heart could wish.

8. They are corrupt, and speak wickedly concern-
-ing oppression: they speak loftily.

9. They set their mouth against the heavens, and
their tongue walketh through the earth.

10. Therefore his people return hither: and waters
of a full cup are wrung out to them.

11. And they say, How doth GOD know? and
is there knowledge in the most HIGH?

12. Behold, these are the ungodly, who prosper in
the world; they increase in riches.

13. Verily, I have cleansed my heart in vain, and
washed my hands in innocency.

14. For all the day long have I been plagued, and
chastened every morning.

15. If I say, I will speak thus; behold, I should of-
-fend against the generation of thy children.

168.

16. When I thought to know this, it was too painful for me;
17. Until I went into the sanctuary of GOD; then understood I their end.
18. Surely thou didst set them in slippery places: thou castedst them down into destruction.
19. How are they brought into desolation, as in a moment! they are utterly consumed with terrors.
20. As a dream when one awaketh; so, O LORD, when thou awakest, thou shalt despise their image.
21. Thus my heart was grieved, and I was pricked in my reins.
22. So foolish was I, and ignorant; I was as a beast before thee.
23. Nevertheless I am continually with thee: thou hast holden me by my right hand.
24. Thou shalt guide me with thy counsel, and afterward receive me to glory.
25. Whom have I in heaven but thee? and there is none upon earth that I desire beside thee.
26. My flesh and my heart faileth: but GOD is the strength of my heart, and my portion for ever.
27. For, lo, they that are far from thee shall perish: thou hast destroyed all them that go a whoring from thee.
28. But it is good for me to draw near to GOD: I have put my trust in the LORD GOD, that I may declare all thy works.

PSALM LXXIV.

Maschil of Asaph.

O GOD, why hast thou cast us off for ever? why doth thine anger smoke against the sheep of thy pasture?
2. Remember thy congregation, which thou hast purchased of old; the rod of thine inheritance,

which thou hast redeemed; this mount **Zion**, wherein thou hast dwelt.

3. **Lift** up thy feet unto the perpetual desolations; *even* all *that* the enemy hath done wickedly in the sanctuary.

4. **Thine** enemies roar in the midst of thy congregations; they set up their ensigns *for* signs.

5. **A** *man* was famous according as he had lifted up axes upon the thick trees.

6. **But** now they break down the carved work thereof at once with axes and hammers.

7. **They** have cast fire into thy sanctuary, they have defiled *by casting down* the dwelling place of thy name to the ground.

8. **They** said in their hearts, Let us destroy them together; they have burned up all the synagogues of **God** in the land.

9. **We** see not our signs: *there is* no more any prophet: neither *is there* among us any that knoweth how long.

10. **O God,** how long shall the adversary reproach? shall the enemy blaspheme thy name for ever?

11. **Why** withdrawest thou thy hand, even thy right hand? pluck *it* out of thy bosom.

12. **For God** *is* my **King** of old, working salva--tion in the midst of the earth.

13. **Thou** didst divide the sea by thy strength: thou brakest the heads of the dragons in the waters.

14. **Thou** brakest the heads of leviathan in pieces, *and gav--est* him to be meat to the people inhabiting the wilderness.

15. **Thou** didst cleave the fountain and the flood: thou dried--est up mighty rivers.

16. **The** day *is* thine, the night also *is* thine: thou hast pre--pared the light and the sun.

17. **Thou** hast set all the borders of the earth: thou hast made summer and winter.

18. **Remember** this, *that* the enemy hath reproached, **O Lord,** and *that* the foolish people have blasphemed thy name.

19. **O** deliver not the soul of thy turtledove unto the multitude *of the wicked:* forget not the

congregation of thy poor for ever.

20. Have respect unto the covenant: for the dark places of the earth are full of the habitations of cruelty.

21. O let not the oppressed return ashamed: let the poor and needy praise thy name.

22. Arise, **O GOD**, plead thine own cause: remember how the foolish man reproacheth thee daily.

23. Forget not the voice of thine enemies: the tumult of those that rise up against thee increaseth continually.

PSALM LXXV.

To the chief Musician, Al-taschith, A Psalm or Song of Asaph.

UNTO thee, **O GOD**, do we give thanks, *unto thee* do we give thanks: for *that* thy name is near thy wondrous works declare.

2. When I shall receive the congregation I will judge uprightly.

3. The earth and all the inhabitants thereof are dissolved: I bear up the pillars of it. **Selah.**

4. I said unto the fools, Deal not foolishly: and to the wicked, Lift not up the horn:

5. Lift not up your horn on high: speak *not with* a stiff neck.

6. For promotion *cometh* neither from the east, nor from the west, nor from the south.

7. But **GOD** *is* the judge: he putteth down one, and setteth up another

8. For in the hand of the **LORD** *there is* a cup, and the wine is red; it is full of mixture; and he poureth out of the same: but the dregs thereof, all the wicked of the earth shall wring *them* out, *and* drink *them*.

9. But I will declare for ever; I will sing praises to the **GOD of Jacob.**

10. All the horns of the wicked also will I cut off *but the* horns of the righteous shall be exalted.

PSALM LXXVI.

To the chief Musician on Neginoth A Psalm
or Song of Asaph.

IN Judah is GOD known: his name is
great in Israel.

2. In Salem also is his tabernacle, and his
dwelling place in Zion.

3. There brake he the arrows of the bow, the shield,
and the sword, and the battle. Selah.

4. Thou art more glorious and excellent than the moun-
-tains of prey.

5. The stouthearted are spoiled, they have slept their sleep:
and none of the men of might have found their
hands.

6. At thy rebuke, O GOD of Jacob, both the cha-
-riot and horse are cast into a dead sleep.

7. Thou, even thou, art to be feared: and who may
stand in thy sight when once thou art angry?

8. Thou didst cause judgement to be heard from heaven;
the earth feared, and was still,

9. When GOD arose to judgement, to save all the
meek of the earth. Selah.

10. Surely the wrath of man shall praise thee: the re-
-mainder of wrath shall thou restrain.

11. Vow, and pay unto the LORD your GOD:
let all that be round about him bring presents
unto him that ought to be feared.

12. He shall cut off the spirit of princes: he is terrible
to the kings of the earth.

PSALM LXXVII.

To the chief Musician, to Jeduthun, A Psalm
of Asaph.

I CRIED unto GOD with my voice, even unto GOD
with my voice; and he gave ear unto me.

2. In the day of my trouble I sought the LORD: my sore ran in the night, and ceased not: my soul refused to be comforted.

3. I remembered GOD, and was troubled: I complained, and my spirit was overwhelmed. Selah.

4. Thou holdest mine eyes waking: I am so troubled that I cannot speak.

5. I have considered the days of old, the years of ancient times.

6. I call to remembrance my song in the night: I commune with mine own heart: and my spirit made diligent search.

7. Will the LORD cast off for ever? and will he be favourable no more?

8. Is his mercy clean gone for ever? doth his promise fail for evermore?

9. Hath GOD forgotten to be gracious? hath he in anger shut up his tender mercies? Selah.

10. And I said, "This is my infirmity: but I will remember the years of the right hand of the most High.

11. I will remember the works of the LORD: surely I will remember thy wonders of old.

12. I will meditate also of all thy work, and talk of thy doings.

13. Thy way O GOD is in the sanctuary: who is so great a GOD as our GOD?

14. Thou art the GOD that doest wonders: thou hast declared thy strength among the people.

15. Thou hast with thine arm redeemed thy people, the sons of Jacob and Joseph. Selah.

16. The waters saw thee, O GOD, the waters saw thee; they were afraid: the depths also were troubled.

17. The clouds poured out water: the skies sent out a sound: thine arrows also went abroad.

18. The voice of thy thunder was in the heaven: the lightnings lightened the world: the earth trembled and shook.

19. Thy way is in the sea, and thy path in the great waters, and thy footsteps are not known.

Thou leddest thy people like a flock by the hand of Moses and Aaron.

PSALM ✳ LXXVIII.

Maschil of Asaph.

GIVE ear, O my people, to my law: incline your ears
to the words of my mouth.

2. I will open my mouth in a parable: I will utter dark
sayings of old:

3. Which we have heard and known, and our fathers have
told us.

4. We will not hide them from their children, shewing to the
generation to come the praises of the LORD, and his
strength, and his wonderful works that he hath done.

5. For he established a testimony in Jacob, and appointed
a law in Israel, which he commanded our fathers,
that they should make them known to their children:

6. That the generation to come might know them, even the
children which should be born; who should arise
and declare them to their children:

7. That they might set their hope in GOD and not for-
-get the works of GOD, but keep his command-
-ments:

8. And might not be as their fathers, a stubborn and re-
-bellious generation; a generation that set not
their heart aright, and whose spirit was not sted-
-fast with GOD.

9. The children of Ephraim, being armed, and car-
-rying bows, turned back in the day of battle.

10. They kept not the covenant of GOD and refused
to walk in his law;

11. And forgat his works, and his wonders that he had
shewed them.

12. Marvellous things did he in the sight of their fa-
-thers, in the land of Egypt, in the field of
Zoan.

13. He divided the sea, and caused them to pass through;
and he made the waters to stand as an heap.

14. In the daytime also he led them with a cloud, and all
the night with a light of fire.

15. He clave the rocks in the wilderness, and gave them
drink as out of the great depths.

16. He brought streams also out of the rock, and caused waters also to run down like rivers.

17. And they sinned yet more against him by provoking the most High in the wilderness.

18. And they tempted GOD in their heart by asking ~~meat~~ meat for their lust.

19. Yea, they spake against GOD; they said, Can GOD furnish a table in the wilderness?

20. Behold, he smote the rock, that the waters gushed out, and the streams overflowed; can he give bread also? can he provide flesh for his people?

21. Therefore the LORD heard this, and was wroth; so a fire was kindled against Jacob, and anger also came up against Israel;

22. Because they believed not in GOD, and trusted not in his salvation.

23. Though he had commanded the clouds from above, and opened the doors of heaven.

24. And had rained down manna upon them to eat, and had given them of the corn of heaven.

25. Man did eat angels' food: he sent them meat to the full.

26. He caused an east wind to blow in the heaven: and by his power he brought in the south wind.

27. He rained flesh also upon them as dust, and feathered fowls like as the sand of the sea:

28. And he let it fall in the midst of their camp, round about their habitations.

29. So they did eat, and were well filled: for he gave them their own desire;

30. They were not estranged from their lust. But while their meat was yet in their mouths,

31. The wrath of GOD came upon them, and slew the fattest of them, and smote down the chosen men of Israel.

32. For all this they sinned still, and believed not for his wondrous works.

33. Therefore their days did he consume in vanity, and their years in trouble.

34. When he slew them, then they sought him: and they returned and enquired early after GOD.

35. And they remembered that GOD was their rock, and the high GOD their redeemer.

36. Nevertheless they did flatter him with their mouth, and they lied unto him with their tongues.

37. For their heart was not right with him, neither were they stedfast in his covenant.

38. But he, being full of compassion, forgave their iniquity, and destroyed them not: yea, many a time turned he his wrath away, and did not stir up all his anger.

39. For he remembered that they were but flesh; a wind that passeth away, and cometh not again.

40. How oft did they provoke him in the wilderness, and grieve him in the desert!

41. Yea, they turned back and tempted GOD, and limited the Holy One of Israel.

42. They remembered not his hand, nor the day when he delivered them from the enemy.

43. How he had wrought his signs in Egypt, and his wonders in the field of Zoan:

44. And had turned their rivers into blood; and their floods, that they could not drink.

45. He sent divers sorts of flies among them, which devoured them; and frogs, which destroyed them.

46. He gave also their increase unto the caterpiller, and their labour unto the locust.

47. He destroyed their vines with hail, and their sycomore trees with frost.

48. He gave up their cattle also to the hail, and their flocks to hot thunderbolts.

49. He cast upon them the fierceness of his anger, wrath, and indignation, and trouble, by sending evil angels among them.

50. He made a way to his anger; he spared not their soul from death, but gave their life over to the pestilence;

51. And smote all the firstborn in Egypt; the chief of their strength in the tabernacles of Ham:

52. But made his own people to go forth like sheep, and guided them in the wilderness like a flock.

53. And he led them on safely, so that they feared not: but the sea overwhelmed their enemies.

54. And he brought them to the border of his sanctuary, even to this mountain, which his right hand had purchased.

55. He cast out the heathen also before them, and divided them an inheritance by line, and made the tribes of Israel to dwell in their tents.

56. Yet they tempted and provoked the most high GOD, and kept not his testimonies:

57. But turned back, and dealt unfaithfully like their fathers: they were turned aside like a deceitful bow.

58. For they provoked him to anger with their high places, and moved him to jealousy with their graven images.

59. When GOD heard this, he was wroth, and greatly abhorred Israel:

60. So that he forsook the tabernacle of Shiloh, the tent which he placed among men;

61. And delivered his strength into captivity, and his glory into the enemy's hand.

62. He gave his people over also unto the sword; and was wroth with his inheritance.

63. The fire consumed their young men; and their maidens were not given to marriage.

64. Their priests fell by the sword; and their widows made no lamentation.

65. Then the LORD awaked as one out of sleep, and like a mighty man that shouteth by reason of wine.

66. And he smote his enemies in the hinder parts: he put them to a perpetual reproach.

67. Moreover he refused the tabernacle of Joseph, and chose not the tribe of Ephraim:

68. But chose the tribe of Judah, the mount Zion which he loved.

69. And he built his sanctuary like high palaces, like the earth which he hath established for ever.

70. He chose David also his servant, and took him from the sheepfolds:

71. From following the ewes great with young he brought him to feed Jacob his people and Israel his inheritance.

72. So he fed them according to the integrity of his heart; and guided them by the skilfulness of his hands.

PSALM LXXIX.

A Psalm of Asaph.

O GOD the heathen are come into thine inheritance; thy holy temple have they defiled: they have laid Jerusalem on heaps.

2. The dead bodies of thy servants have they given to be meat unto the fowls of the heaven, the flesh of thy saints unto the beasts of the earth.

3. Their blood have they shed like water round about Jerusalem; and there was none to bury them.

4. We are become a reproach to our neighbours, a scorn and derision to them that are round about us.

5. How long LORD? wilt thou be angry for ever? shall thy jealousy burn like fire?

6. Pour out thy wrath upon the heathen that have not known thee, and upon the kingdoms that have not called upon thy name.

7. For they have devoured Jacob, and laid waste his dwelling place.

8. O remember not against us former iniquities: let thy tender mercies speedily prevent us: for we are brought very low.

9. Help us, O GOD of our salvation, for the glory of thy name: and deliver us, and purge away our sins, for thy name's sake.

10. Wherefore should the heathen say, Where is their GOD? let him be known among the heathen in our sight by the revenging of the blood of thy servants which is shed.

11. Let the sighing of the prisoner come before thee, according to the greatness of thy power preserve thou those that are appointed to die.

12. And render unto our neighbours sevenfold into their bosom their reproach, wherewith they have reproached thee, O LORD.

13. So we thy people and sheep of thy pasture will give thee thanks for ever: we will show forth thy praise to all generations.

PSALM LXXX.

To the chief Musician upon Shoshannim Eduth,
A Psalm of Asaph.

GIVE ear, O Shepherd of Israel, thou that leadest
Joseph like a flock; thou that dwellest between the
cherubims, shine forth.

2. Before Ephraim and Benjamin and Manasseh stir
up thy strength, and come and save us.

3. Turn us again, O GOD, and cause thy face to shine; and
we shall be saved.

4. O LORD GOD of hosts, how long wilt thou be angry
against the prayer of thy people?

5. Thou feedest them with the bread of tears: and givest them tears
to drink in great measure.

6. Thou makest us a strife unto our neighbours: and our enemies
laugh among themselves.

7. Turn us again, O GOD of hosts, and cause thy face
to shine; and we shall be saved.

8. Thou hast brought a vine out of Egypt: thou hast cast out
the heathen, and planted it.

9. Thou preparedst room before it, and didst cause it to take deep
root, and it filled the land.

10. The hills were covered with the shadow of it, and the boughs
thereof were like the goodly cedars.

11. She sent out her boughs unto the sea, and her branches unto
the river.

12. Why hast thou then broken down her hedges, so that all they
which pass by the way do pluck her?

13. The boar out of the wood doth waste it, and the wild beast of
the field doth devour it.

14. Return, we beseech thee, O GOD of hosts: look down
from heaven, and behold, and visit this vine;

15. And the vineyard which thy right hand hath planted, and the
branch that thou madest strong for thyself.

16. It is burned with fire, it is cut down: they perish at the re-
-buke of thy countenance.

17. Let thy hand be upon the man of thy right hand, upon the son of man whom thou madest strong for thyself.

18. So will not we go back from thee: quicken us, and we will call upon thy name.

19. Turn us again, **O LORD GOD** of hosts, cause thy face to shine; and we shall be saved.

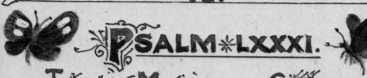

PSALM ✻ LXXXI.

To the chief Musician upon Gittith.
A Psalm of Asaph.

SING aloud unto **GOD** our strength: make a joyful noise unto the **GOD** of **Jacob**.

2. Take a psalm, and bring hither the timbrel, the pleasant harp with the psaltery.

3. Blow up the trumpet in the new moon, in the time appointed, on our solemn feast day.

4. For this was a statute for **Israel**, and a law of the **GOD** of **Jacob**.

5. This he ordained in **Joseph** for a testimony, when he went out through the land of **Egypt**: where I heard a language that I understood not.

6. I removed his shoulder from the burden: his hands were delivered from the pots.

7. Thou calledst in trouble, and I delivered thee; I answered thee in the secret place of thunder: I proved thee at the waters of **Meribah**. **Selah**.

8. Hear, O my people, and I will testify unto thee: O **Israel**, if thou wilt hearken unto me.

9. There shall no strange god be in thee: neither shalt thou worship any strange god.

10. I am the **LORD** thy **GOD**; which brought thee out of the land of **Egypt**: open thy mouth wide, and I will fill it.

11. But my people would not hearken to my voice; and Israel would none of me.

12. So I gave them up unto their own hearts' lust: and they walk-ed in their own counsels.

13. O that my people had hearkened unto me, and Israel had walked in my ways!

14. I should soon have subdued their enemies, and turned my hand against their adversaries.

15. The haters of the LORD should have submitted themselves unto him: but their time should have endured for ever.

16. He should have fed them also with the finest of the wheat: and with honey out of the rock should I have satisfied thee.

PSALM LXXXII.

A Psalm of Asaph.

GOD standeth in the congregation of the mighty: he judgeth among the gods.

2. How long will ye judge unjustly, and accept the persons of the wicked? Selah.

3. Defend the poor and fatherless: do justice to the afflicted and needy.

4. Deliver the poor and needy: rid them out of the hand of the wicked.

5. They know not, neither will they understand; they walk on in darkness: all the foundations of the earth are out of course.

6. I have said, Ye are gods; and all of you are children of the most High.

7. But ye shall die like men, and fall like one of the princes.

8. Arise, O GOD, judge the earth: for thou shalt inherit all nations.

3

PSALM * LXXXIII.

A Song or Psalm of Asaph.

KEEP not thou silence, O GOD: hold not thy peace, and be not still, O GOD.

2. For, lo, thine enemies make a tumult: and they that hate thee have lifted up the head.

3. They have taken crafty counsel against thy people, and consulted against thy hidden ones.

4. They have said, Come, and let us cut them off from being a nation; so that the name of Israel may be no more in remembrance.

5. For they have consulted together with one consent: they are confederate against thee:

6. The tabernacles of Edom, and the Ishmaelites; of Moab, and the Hagarenes:

7. Gebal, and Ammon, and Amalek; the Philistines with the inhabitants of Tyre;

8. Assur also is joined with them: they have holpen the children of Lot. Selah.

9. Do unto them as unto the Midianites; as to Sisera, as to Jabin. at the brook of Kison.

10. Which perished at Endor: they became as dung for the earth

11. Make their nobles like Oreb, and like Zeeb: yea, all their princes as Zebah, and as Zalmunna:

12. Who said, Let us take to ourselves the houses of GOD in possession

13. O my GOD, make them like a wheel; as the stubble before the wind.

14. As the fire burneth a wood, and as the flame setteth the mountains on fire;

15. So persecute them with thy tempest, and make them afraid with thy storm.

16. Fill their faces with shame: that they may seek thy name, O LORD.

17. Let them be confounded and troubled for ever; yea, let them be put to shame, and perish:

18. That men may know that thou, whose name alone is

JEHOVAH,

art the most high over all the earth.

PSALM LXXXIV.

To the chief Musician upon Gittith. A Psalm for the sons of Korah.

How amiable are thy tabernacles, **O LORD of hosts!**

2. My soul longeth, yea, even fainteth for the courts of the LORD: my heart and my flesh crieth out for the living GOD.

3. Yea, the sparrow hath found an house, and the swallow a nest for herself, where she may lay her young, even thine altars, **O LORD of hosts, my King, and my GOD.**

4. Blessed are they that dwell in thy house: they will be still praising thee. Selah.

5. Blessed is the man whose strength is in thee, in whose heart are the ways of them.

6. Who passing through the valley of Baca make it a well: the rain also filleth the pools.

7. They go from strength to strength. every one of them in Zion appeareth before GOD.

8. O LORD GOD of hosts, hear my prayer: give ear, O GOD of Jacob. Selah.

9. Behold, O GOD our shield, and look upon the face of thine anointed.

10. For a day in thy courts is better than a thousand.
I had rather be a doorkeeper in the
HOUSE OF MY GOD,
than to dwell in the tents of wickedness.

11. For The Lord God is a Sun
and Shield: the LORD will give
Grace and Glory:
no good thing will he withhold from
them that walk uprightly.

12. O LORD of hosts, blessed
is the man
that trusteth in thee.

PSALM LXXXV.

To the chief Musician. A Psalm for the
sons of Korah.

LORD, thou hast been favourable unto thy land: thou
hast brought back the captivity of Jacob.
2. Thou hast forgiven the iniquity of thy people. Thou
hast covered all their sin. Selah:

3. Thou hast taken away all thy wrath: thou hast turned thyself
from the fierceness of thine anger.

4. Turn us, O GOD of our Salvation. and cause thine anger
toward us to cease.

5. Will thou be angry with us for ever? will thou draw out
thine anger to all generations?

6. Will thou not revive us again: that thy people may rejoice
in thee?

7. Shew us thy mercy; O LORD, and grant us
thy Salvation.

8. I will hear what GOD the LORD will speak: for he
will speak peace unto his people, and to his saints:
but let them not turn again to folly.

9. Surely his Salvation is nigh them that fear him; that
glory may dwell in our land.

10. Mercy and truth are met together; righteousness and peace
have kissed each other.

11. Truth shall spring out of the earth; and righteousness shall
look down from heaven.

12. Yea, the LORD shall give that which is good; and our land
shall yield her increase.

13. Righteousness shall go before him: and shall set
us in the way of his steps.

PSALM LXXXVI.

A Prayer of David.

BOW down thine ear, O LORD, hear me:
for I am poor and needy.

2. Preserve my soul; for I am holy: O thou
MY GOD,
save thy servant that trusteth in thee.

3. Be merciful unto me, O LORD:
for I cry unto thee daily.

4. Rejoice the soul of thy servant: for
unto thee, O LORD,
do I lift up my soul.

5. For thou, LORD, art good,
and ready to forgive;
and plenteous in mercy —
unto all them that call upon thee,

6. Give ear, O LORD, unto my prayer;
and attend to the voice of my supplications.

7. In the day of my trouble I will call upon thee:
for thou wilt answer me.

8. Among the gods there is none like unto thee, O LORD;
neither are there any works like unto thy works.

9. All nations whom thou hast made shall come
and worship before thee, O LORD; and
shall GLORIFY THY NAME.

10. For thou art great, and doest wondrous
things: thou art GOD alone.

11. Teach me thy way, O LORD;
I will walk in thy truth: unite my
heart to fear thy name.

12. I will praise thee, O LORD my GOD, with all my heart: and I will glorify thy name for evermore.

13. For great is thy mercy toward me: and thou hast delivered my soul from the lowest hell.

14. O GOD, the proud are risen against me: and the assemblies of violent men have sought after my soul; and have not set thee before them.

15. But thou, O LORD, art a GOD full of compassion, and gracious, longsuffering, and plenteous in mercy and truth.

16. O turn unto me, and have mercy upon me; give thy strength unto thy servant, and save the son of thine handmaid.

17. Shew me a token for good; that they which hate me may see it, and be ashamed: because thou, LORD, hast holpen me, and comforted me.

PSALM LXXXVII.

A Psalm or Song for the sons of Korah.

HIS foundation is in the holy mountains.

2. The LORD loveth the gates of Zion more than all dwellings of Jacob.

3. Glorious things are spoken of thee, O city of GOD. Selah.

4. I will make mention of Rahab and Babylon to them that know me: behold Philistia, and Tyre, with Ethiopia; this man was born there.

5. And of Zion it shall be said, This and that man was born in her: and the highest himself shall establish her.

6. The LORD shall count, when he writeth up the people, that this man was born there. Selah.

7. As well the singers as the players on instruments shall be there: all my springs are in thee.

PSALM LXXXVIII.

To the chief Musician upon Mahalath Leannoth, Maschil of Heman the Ezrahite.
A Song or Psalm for the sons of Korah.

O LORD GOD of my salvation, I have cried day and night before thee:

2. Let my prayer come before thee: incline thine ear unto my cry;

3. For my soul is full of troubles: and my life draweth nigh unto the grave.

4. I am counted with them that go down into the pit: I am as a man that hath no strength:

5. Free among the dead, like the slain that lie in the grave, whom thou rememberest no more: and they are cut off from thy hand.

6. Thou hast laid me in the lowest pit, in darkness, in the deeps.

7. Thy wrath lieth hard upon me, and thou hast afflicted me with all thy waves. Selah.

8. Thou hast put away mine acquaintance far from me: thou hast made me an abomination unto them: I am shut up, and I cannot come forth.

9. Mine eye mourneth by reason of affliction; Lord, I have called daily upon thee, I have stretched out my hands unto thee.

10. Wilt thou shew wonders to the dead? shall the dead arise and praise thee? Selah

11. Shall thy lovingkindness be declared in the grave? or thy faithfulness in destruction?

12. Shall thy wonders be known in the dark? and thy righteousness in the land of forgetfulness?

13. But unto thee have I cried, O LORD; and in the morning shall my prayer prevent thee.

14. LORD, why castest thou off my soul? why hidest thou thy face from me?

15. I am afflicted and ready to die from my youth up; while I suffer thy terrors I am distracted.

16. Thy fierce wrath goeth over me; thy terrors have cut me off.

17. They came round about me daily like water; they com--passed me about together.

18. Lover and friend hast thou put far from me, and mine acquaintance into darkness.

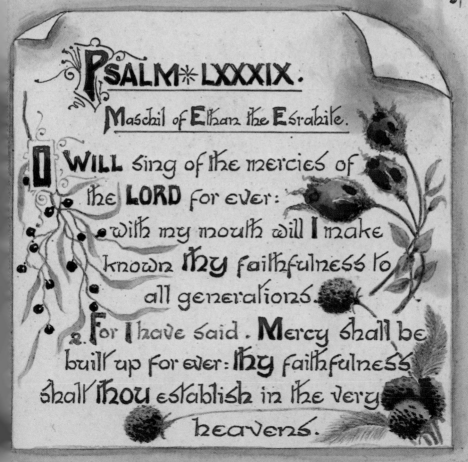

Psalm LXXXIX.

Maschil of Ethan the Esrahite.

O WILL sing of the mercies of the LORD for ever: with my mouth will I make known thy faithfulness to all generations.

2. For I have said. Mercy shall be built up for ever: thy faithfulness shall thou establish in the very heavens.

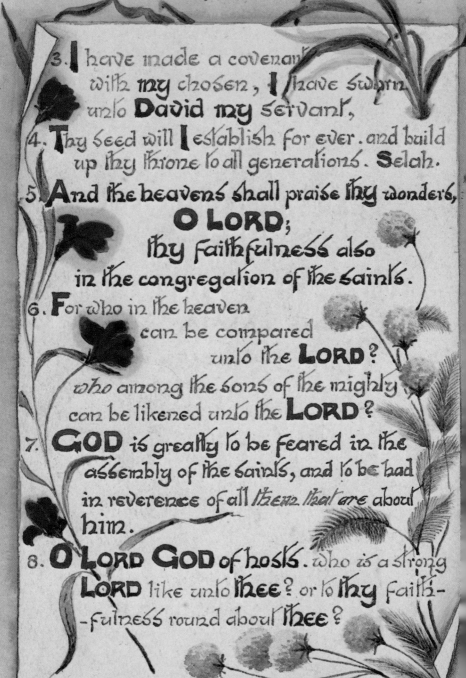

3. I have made a covenant with **my chosen**, I have sworn unto **David my servant**,

4. **Thy** seed will I establish for ever, and build up thy throne to all generations. **Selah**.

5. **And the heavens shall praise thy wonders, O LORD;** thy faithfulness also in the congregation of the saints.

6. For who in the heaven can be compared unto the **LORD**? who among the sons of the mighty can be likened unto the **LORD**?

7. **GOD** is greatly to be feared in the assembly of the saints, and to be had in reverence of all *them that are* about **him**.

8. **O LORD GOD** of hosts. who is a strong **LORD** like unto **thee**? or to **thy** faith- -fulness round about **thee**?

9. Thou rulest the raging of the sea: when the waves thereof arise, thou stillest them.

10. Thou hast broken Rahab in pieces, as one that is slain; thou hast scattered thine ene- -mies with thy strong arm.

11. The heavens are thine. the earth also is thine: as for the world and the fulness thereof, thou hast founded them.

12. The north and the south thou hast created them: Tabor and Hermon shall rejoice in thy name.

13. Thou hast a mighty arm: strong is thy hand, and high is thy right hand.

14. Justice and judgement are the habitation of thy throne: mercy and truth shall go before thy face.

15. Blessed is the people that know the joyful sound: they shall walk, O LORD, in the light of thy countenance.

16. In thy name shall they rejoice all the day: and in thy righteousness shall they be exalted.

17. For thou art the glory of their strength: and in thy favour our horn shall be exalted.

18. For The Lord is our defence: and The Holy One of Israel is our King.

19. Then thou spakest in vision to thy holy one, and saidst: I have laid help upon one that is mighty; I have exalted one chosen out of the people.

20. I have found David my servant; with my holy oil have I anointed him:

21. With whom my hand shall be established: mine arm also shall strengthen him.

22. The enemy shall not exact upon him; nor the son of wickedness afflict him.

23. And I will beat down his foes before his face, and plague them that hate him.

24. But my faithfulness and my mercy shall be with him: and in my name shall his horn be exalted.

25. I will set his hand also in the sea, and his right hand in the rivers.

26. He shall cry unto me,

Thou art my Father, my God,

and the rock of my salvation.

27. Also I will make him my firstborn, higher than the kings of the earth.

28. My mercy will I keep for him for evermore, and my covenant shall stand fast with him.

29. His seed also will I make to endure for ever, and his throne as the days of heaven.

30. If his children forsake my law, and walk not in my judgments;

31. If they break my statutes, and keep not my commandments:

32. Then will I visit their transgression with the rod, and their iniquity with stripes.

33. Nevertheless my lovingkindness will I not utterly take from him, nor suffer my faithfulness to fail.

34. My covenant will I not break, nor alter the thing that is gone out of my lips.

35. Once have I sworn by my holiness that I will not lie unto David.

36. His seed shall endure for ever, and his throne as the sun before me.

37. It shall be established for ever as the moon, and as a faithful witness in heaven. Selah

38. But thou hast cast off and abhored, thou hast been wroth with thine anointed.

39. Thou hast made void the covenant of thy servant: thou hast profaned his crown by casting it to the ground.

40. **Thou** hast broken down all his hedges; thou hast brought his strongholds to ruin.

41. **All** that pass by the way spoil him: he is a reproach to his neighbours.

42. **Thou** hast set up the right hand of his adversaries; thou hast made all his enemies to rejoice.

43. **Thou** hast also turned the edge of his sword, and hast not made him to stand in the battle.

44. **Thou** hast made his glory to cease, and cast his throne down to the ground.

45. **The** days of his youth hast **thou** shortened: **thou** hast covered him with shame. Selah.

46. **How** long, **LORD**? wilt **thou** hide **thyself** for ever? shall **thy** wrath burn like fire?

47. **Remember** how short my time is: wherefore hast **thou** made all men in vain?

48. **What** man is he that liveth, and shall not see death? shall he deliver his soul from the hand of the grave? Selah.

49. **LORD**, where are **thy** lovingkindnesses, which **thou** swarest unto David in **thy** truth?

50. Remember, **LORD**, the reproach of thy ser-
-vants: how I do bear in my bosom the re-
-proach of all the mighty people;

51. Wherewith **thine** enemies have reproached,
O LORD; wherewith they have reproached
the footsteps of **thine** anointed.

52. Blessed be the Lord for

evermore.

Amen, and Amen.

PSALM · XC.

A Prayer of Moses the man of GOD.

LORD, thou hast been
our dwelling place
in all generations.

2. Before the mountains were brought forth, or ever
thou hadst formed the earth and the world,

.:.

even from everlasting
to everlasting
thou art GOD.

3. Thou turnest man to destruction;
and sayest, Return, ye children of men.

4. For a thousand years in thy sight
are but as yesterday when it is past,
and as a watch in the night.

5. Thou carriest them away as with a flood; they
are as a sleep: in the morning they are like grass
which groweth up.

6. In the morning it flourisheth, and groweth up; in
the evening it is cut down, and withereth.

7. For we are consumed by thine anger. and by thy
wrath are we troubled.

8. Thou hast set our iniquities before thee, our
secret sins in the light of thy countenance.

9. For all our days are passed away in thy wrath:
we spend our years as a tale that is told.

10. The days of our years are threescore years and ten;
and if by reason of strength they be fourscore
years, yet is their strength labour and sorrow;
for it is soon cut off,
and we fly away.

11. Who knoweth the power of thine anger? even according to thy fear, so is thy wrath.

12. So teach us to number our days; that we may apply our hearts unto wisdom.

13. Return, O LORD, how long? and let it repent thee concerning thy servants.

14. O satisfy us early with thy mercy; that we may rejoice — and be glad all our days.

15. Make us glad according to the days wherein thou hast afflicted us, and the years wherein we have seen evil.

16. Let thy work appear unto thy servants. and thy glory unto their children.

17. And let the beauty of the LORD our GOD be upon us: and establish thou the work of our hands upon us; yea, the work of our hands establish thou it.

PSALM·XCI.

He that dwelleth in the secret place
of the most **High** shall abide
under the shadow of
the Almighty.

2. I will say of the **LORD**,
He is my refuge,
and my **fortress**:
my **God**;
in **Him** will **I** trust.

3. **Surely he** shall deliver thee from the snare
of the fowler, *and* from the noisome
pestilence.

4. **He** shall cover thee with **his** feathers, *and*
under **his** wings shalt thou trust:
his TRUTH shall be thy
SHIELD and **BUCKLER**.

5. Thou shalt not be afraid for the terror by night;
nor for the arrow *that flieth* by day;

6. **N**or for the pestilence that walketh in darkness; nor for the destruction that wasteth at noonday.

7. **A** thousand shall fall at thy side, and ten thousand at thy right hand; but it shall not come nigh thee.

8. **O**nly with thine eyes shalt thou behold and see the reward of the wicked.

9. **B**ecause thou hast made the **LORD**, which is my refuge, even the most **High**. thy habit-ation;

10. **T**here shall no evil befall thee, neither shall any plague come nigh thy dwelling.

11. For **He shall give his angels charge over thee, to keep thee in all thy ways.**

12. **They** shall bear thee up in their hands, lest thou dash thy foot against a stone.

13. **Thou** shalt tread upon the lion and adder: the young lion and the dragon shalt thou trample under feet.

14. **B**ecause he hath set his love upon **ME**, therefore will **I** deliver him: I will set him on high, because he hath known **MY NAME**.

15. He shall call upon ME,
and I will answer him:
I will be with him in trouble,
I will deliver him,
and honour him.

16. With long life will I satisfy him,
and shew him MY salvation.

PSALM*XCII.

A Psalm or Song for the sabbath day

IT is a good thing to give thanks
unto the LORD,
and to sing praises
unto thy name,
O most HIGH:

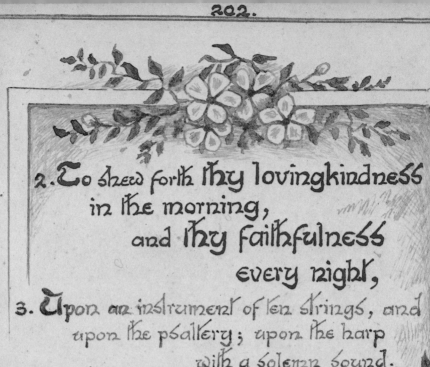

2. To shew forth thy lovingkindness in the morning,
     and thy faithfulness
          every night,

3. Upon an instrument of ten strings, and upon the psaltery; upon the harp with a solemn sound.

4. For thou, LORD, hast made me glad through thy work: I will triumph in the works of thy hands.

5. O LORD, how great are thy works! and thy thoughts are very deep.

6. A brutish man knoweth not; neither doth a fool understand this.

7. When the wicked spring as the grass, and when all the workers of iniquity do flourish; it is that they shall be destroyed for ever.

8. But thou, **LORD**,
    art most high for evermore.
9. For, lo, thine enemies, **O LORD**, for, lo,
    thine enemies shall perish; all the
    workers of iniquity shall be scattered.
10. But my horn shall **thou** exalt like *the*
    horn of an unicorn : I shall be anointed
    with fresh oil.
11. Mine eye also shall see *my desire* on mine
    enemies, *and* mine ears shall hear *my de-*
    -sire of the wicked that rise up against me.
12. The righteous shall flourish like the palm tree:
    he shall grow like a cedar in **Lebanon**.
13. Those that be planted in the house of the
    LORD shall flourish in the courts of
    our **GOD**.
14. They shall still bring forth fruit in old
    age; they shall be fat and flourishing;
15. To shew that the **LORD** is upright:

He is my rock,
    and *there is*
no unrighteousness in **him**.

PSALM * XCIII.

THE LORD reigneth,
  He is clothed with majesty;
the LORD is clothed with strength,
  wherewith He hath girded Himself:
    the world also is stablished,
      that it cannot be moved.

2. Thy throne is established of old:
    thou art from everlasting.

3. The floods have lifted up, O LORD, the
    floods have lifted up their voice;
  the floods lift up their waves.

4. The LORD on high is mightier than the
    noise of many waters, yea than the
  mighty waves of the sea.

5. Thy testimonies are very sure:
    holiness becometh Thine house,
      O LORD. for ever.

PSALM XCIV.

O LORD GOD, to whom vengeance belongeth; O GOD, to whom vengeance belongeth, shew thyself.

2. Lift up thyself, thou judge of the earth: render a reward to the proud.

3 LORD, how long shall the wicked, how long shall the wicked triumph?

4. How long shall they utter and speak hard things? and all the workers of iniquity boast themselves?

5. They break in pieces thy people, O LORD, and afflict thine heritage.

6. They slay the widow and the stranger, and murder the fatherless.

7. Yet they say, The LORD shall not see, neither shall the GOD of Jacob regard it.

8. Understand, ye brutish among the people: and ye fools, when will ye be wise?

9. He that planted the ear, shall he not hear? he that formed the eye, shall he not see?

10. He that chastiseth the heathen, shall not he correct? he that teacheth man knowledge, shall not he know?

11. The LORD knoweth the thoughts of man, that they are vanity.

12. **Blessed** *is* the man whom **Thou** chastenest, **O LORD**, and teachest him out of **thy** law:

13. That **thou** mayest give him rest from the days of adversity, until the pit be digged for the wicked.

14. For the **LORD** will not cast off **his** people, neither will **he** forsake **his** inheritance.

15. But judgment shall return unto righteousness: and all the upright in heart shall follow it.

16. **Who** will rise up for me against the evildoers? *or* who will stand up for me against the workers of iniquity?

17. **Unless** the **LORD** had been my help, my soul had almost dwelt in silence.

18. **When I** said, **My** foot slippeth; **thy** mercy, **O LORD,** held me up.

19. In the multitude of my thoughts
within me —
Thy comforts delight my soul.

20. Shall the throne of iniquity have fellowship
with thee, which frameth mischief
by a law?

21. They gather themselves together against the
soul of the righteous, and condemn the
innocent blood.

22. But the LORD is my defence;
and
my GOD is the rock
of my refuge.

23. And he shall bring upon them their own
iniquity, and shall cut them off in their
own wickedness; yea,
the LORD our GOD shall cut them off.

PSALM · XCV.

VENITE, EXULTEMUS DOMINO.

O COME, let us sing unto the LORD: let us make a joyful noise to the rock of our salvation.

2. Let us come before **his** presence with thanksgiving, and make a joyful noise unto **him** with psalms.

3. For the **LORD** *is* a great **GOD**, and a great **KING** above all gods.

4. In **his** hand *are* the deep places of the earth: and the strength of the hills *is* **his** also.

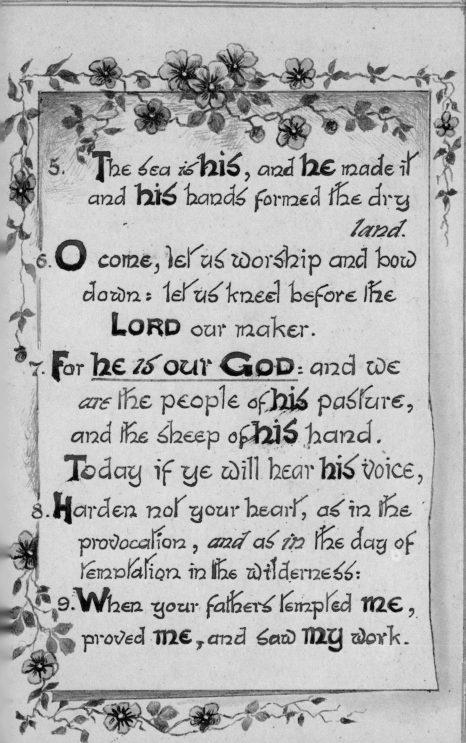

5. The sea is **his**, and **he** made it
and **his** hands formed the dry
land.

6. **O** come, let us worship and bow
down: let us kneel before the
LORD our maker.

7. For **he is our GOD**: and we
are the people of **his** pasture,
and the sheep of **his** hand.
Today if ye will hear **his** voice,

8. **H**arden not your heart, as in the
provocation, *and as in* the day of
temptation in the wilderness:

9. **W**hen your fathers tempted **me**,
proved **me**, and saw **my** work.

10. Forty years long was I grieved with this generation, and said, it is a people that do err in their heart, and they have not known MY ways

11. Unto whom I sware in MY wrath that they should not enter into MY rest.

PSALM XCVI.

O SING unto the LORD a new song: sing unto the LORD, all the earth.

2. Sing unto the LORD, bless his name; shew forth his salvation from day to day.

3. Declare his glory among the heathen, his wonders among all people

4. For the LORD is great, —

and greatly to be praised; **he** *is to be* feared above all gods.

5. For all the gods of the nations *are* idols: but the **LORD** made the heavens.

6. Honour and majesty *are* before **him**: strength and beauty *are* in **his** sanctuary.

7. Give unto the **LORD, O** ye kindreds of the people, give unto the **LORD** glory and strength.

8. Give unto the **LORD** the glory *due unto* **his name**: bring an offering. and come into **his** courts.

9. O worship the **LORD** in the beauty of holiness: fear before **him**, all the earth.

10. Say among the heathen *that* **the LORD reigneth**: the world also shall be established that it shall not be moved: **he shall judge the people righteously.**

11. Let the heavens rejoice, and let the earth be glad; let the sea roar, and the fulness thereof.

12. Let the field be joyful, and all that is therein: then shall all the trees of the wood rejoice

13. Before the LORD:
for HE cometh,
for HE cometh to judge the earth:
HE shall judge the world with
righteousness,
and the people with HIS truth.

PSALM ✱ XCVII.

The LORD reigneth; let the earth rejoice; let the multitude of isles be glad *thereof.*

2. Clouds and darkness are round about him : righteousness and judgment are the habitation of his throne.

3. A fire goeth before him , and burneth up his enemies round about.

4. HIS lightnings enlightened the world; the earth saw, and trembled.

5. The hills melted like wax at the presence of the LORD , at the presence of the LORD of the whole earth.

6. The heavens declare his righteousness, and all the people see his glory.

7. Confounded be all they that serve graven images, that boast themselves of idols: worship him , all ye gods.

8. ZION heard, and was glad; and the daughters of JUDAH rejoiced because of thy judgments , O LORD.

9. For thou , LORD, art high above all the earth:

Thou art exalted far above all gods.

10. Ye that love the **LORD** hate evil: **he** preserveth the souls of **his** saints; **he** delivereth them out of the hand of the wicked.

11. Light is sown for the righteous, and gladness for the upright in heart.

12. Rejoice in the **LORD**, ye righteous; and give thanks at the remembrance of his holiness.

PSALM ✷ XCVIII.

A Psalm.

CANTATE DOMINO.

O SING unto the **LORD** a new song; for **he** hath done marvellous things.

his right hand, and his holy arm,
hath gotten him the victory.

2. The LORD hath made known
his salvation:
his righteousness
hath HE openly shewed in the
sight of the heathen.

3. HE hath remembered his mercy and
his truth toward the house
of ISRAEL:
all the ends of the earth have seen the
salvation of our GOD.

4. Make a joyful noise unto the LORD, all
the earth: make a loud noise, and re-
-joice, and sing praise.

5. Sing unto the LORD with the harp; with
the harp, and the voice of a psalm.

6. With trumpets and sound of cornet make
a joyful noise before the LORD,
the KING.

7. Let the sea roar, and the fulness thereof; the world, and they that dwell therein.

8. Let the floods clap *their* hands: let the hills be joyful together

9. Before the **LORD**; for **HE** cometh to judge the earth: with **RIGHTEOUSNESS** shall **HE** judge the world, and the people with equity.

PSALM XCIX.

THE LORD reigneth; let the people tremble: **HE** sitteth *between* the cherubims; let the earth be moved.

2. The **LORD** *is* great in **ZION**: and **HE** *is* high above all the people.

3. Let them praise **THY** great and terrible name; *for it is* holy.

4. The king's strength also loveth judgment; thou dost establish equity, thou executest judg--ment and righteousness in JACOB.

5. Exalt ye the LORD our GOD, and worship at his footstool: for he is holy.

6. MOSES and AARON among his priests, and SAMUEL among them that call up-on his name; they called upon the LORD, and he answered them.

7. HE spake unto them in the cloudy pillar: they kept his testimonies, and the ordinance that he gave them.

8. Thou answeredst them,
O LORD our GOD:
thou wast a GOD that forgavest them, though thou tookest vengeance of their inventions.

9. Exalt the LORD our GOD, and worship at his holy hill; for the LORD our GOD is holy.

PSALM C.

A Psalm of Praise.

JUBILATE DEO.

MAKE a joyful noise
unto the **LORD**,
all ye lands.

2. Serve the **LORD**
with gladness:
come before
his presence
with singing.

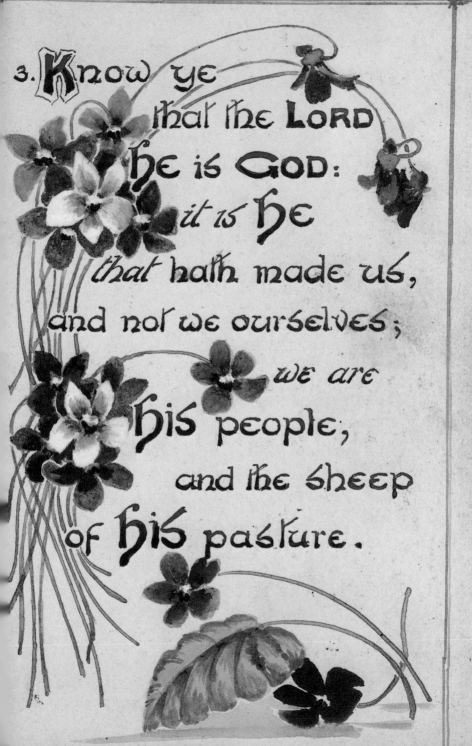

3. Know ye that the LORD he is GOD: it is HE that hath made us, and not we ourselves; we are His people, and the sheep of His pasture.

4. Enter into **His** gates
with thanksgiving
and into **His** courts
with praise:
be thankful unto **him**,
and bless **His** name.

5. For the **LORD** *is* good;
His mercy
is everlasting;
and **His** truth
endureth
to all generations.

HYMN 166.
OLD HUNDREDTH.

"O be joyful in the LORD, all ye lands."

All people that on earth do dwell,
　Sing to the LORD with cheerful voice;
Him serve with fear, His praise forth tell,
　Come ye before Him, and rejoice.

The LORD, ye know, is GOD indeed;
　Without our aid He did us make;
We are His flock, He doth us feed.
　And for His sheep, He doth us take.

O enter then His gates with praise,
　Approach with joy His courts unto;
Praise, laud, and bless His NAME always,
　For it is seemly so to do.

For why? the LORD our GOD is good;
His mercy is for ever sure;
His truth at all times firmly stood,
And shall from age to age endure.

To FATHER, SON. and HOLY GHOST,
The GOD Whom Heav'n and earth adore.
From men and from the Angel-host
Be praise and glory evermore.

PSALM * CI.

A Psalm of David.

I will sing of mercy and judgment: unto thee, O Lord, will I sing.

2. I will behave myself wisely in a perfect way, O when wilt thou come unto me? I will walk within my house with a perfect heart.

3. I will set no wicked thing before mine eyes: I hate the work of them that turn aside; it shall not cleave to me.

4. A froward heart shall depart from me: I will not know a wicked person.

5. Whoso privily slandereth his neighbour, him will I cut off : him that hath an high look and a proud heart will not I suffer.

6. Mine eyes *shall be* upon the faithful of the land, that they may dwell with me : he that walketh in a perfect way, he shall serve me.

7. He that worketh deceit shall not dwell within my house : he that telleth lies shall not tarry in my sight

8. I will early destroy all the wicked of the land; that I may cut off all wicked doers from the city of the LORD.

PSALM ✳ CII.

A Prayer of the afflicted, when he is overwhelmed, and poureth out his complaint before the LORD.

Hear my prayer, O LORD, and let my cry come unto thee.

2. Hide not thy face from me in the day when I am in trouble; incline thine ear unto me: in the day when I call answer me speedily.

3. For my days are consumed like smoke, and my bones are burned as an hearth.

4. My heart is smitten, and withered like grass; so that I forget to eat my bread.

5. By reason of the voice of my groaning my bones cleave to my skin.

6. I am like a pelican of the wilderness; I am like an owl of the desert.

7. I watch, and am as a sparrow alone upon the house top.

8. Mine enemies reproach me all the day; and they that are mad against me are sworn against me.

9. For I have eaten ashes like bread, and mingled my drink with weeping.

10. Because of thine indignation and thy wrath: for thou hast lifted me up, and cast me down.

11. My days are like a shadow that declineth; and I am withered like grass.

12. But thou, O LORD, shalt endure for ever: and thy remembrance unto all generations.

13. Thou shall arise, *and* have mercy upon Zion: for the time to favour her, yea, the set time, is come.

14. For thy servants take pleasure in her stones, and favour the dust thereof.

15. So the heathen shall fear the name of the LORD, and all the kings of the earth thy glory.

16. When the LORD shall build up Zion, he shall appear in his glory.

17. He will regard the prayer of the destitute, and not despise their prayer.

18. This shall be written for the generation to come: and the people which shall be created shall praise the LORD.

19. For he hath looked down from the height of his sanctuary; from heaven did the LORD behold the earth;

20. To hear the groaning of the prisoner; to loose those that are appointed to death;

21. To declare the name of the LORD in Zion. and his praise in Jerusalem;

22. When the people are gathered together, and the kingdoms, to serve the LORD.

23. He weakened my strength in the way: He shortened my days.

24. I said, O my GOD, take me not away in the
midst of my days: thy years are throughout
all generations.

25. Of old hast thou laid the foundation of the earth:
and the heavens are the work of thy hands.

26. They shall perish, but thou shalt endure: yea,
all of them shall wax old like a garment; as a
vesture shalt thou change them, and they shall
be changed.

27. But thou art the same, and thy years shall
have no end.

28. The children of thy servants shall continue,
and their seed shall be established before thee.

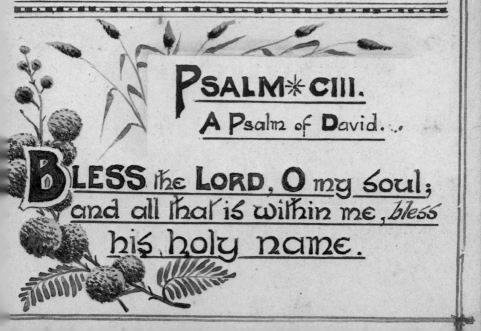

PSALM * CIII.

A Psalm of David.

BLESS the LORD, O my soul;
and all that is within me, *bless*
his holy name.

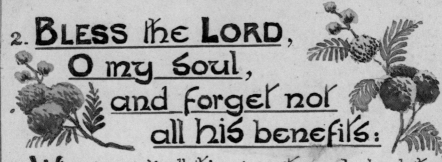

2. **Bless the Lord,**
   O my soul,
   and forget not
   all his benefits:

3. Who forgiveth all thine iniquities : who healeth all thy diseases;

4. Who redeemeth thy life from destruction ; who crown--eth thee with lovingkindness and tender mercies;

5. Who satisfieth thy mouth with good *things*; so that thy youth is renewed like the eagle's.

6. The **Lord** executeth righteousness and judgment for all that are oppressed.

7. **He** made known **his** ways unto **Moses**, **his** acts unto the children of **Israel**.

8. **The Lord *is* merciful**
   and gracious,
   slow to anger,
   and plenteous in mercy.

9. **He** will not always chide : neither will **he** keep *his* anger for ever.

10. **He** hath not dealt with us after our sins : nor re--warded us according to our iniquities.

11. For as the heaven is high above the earth , so great is **his** mercy toward them that fear **him**.

12. As far as the east is from the west, so far hath **he** removed our transgressions from us.

13. Like as a father pitieth *his* children, *so* the **LORD** pitieth them that fear him.

14. For **he** knoweth our frame; **he** remembereth that we *are* dust.

15. *As* for man, his days *are* as grass : as a flower of the field, so he flourisheth.

16. For the wind passeth over it, and it is gone : and the place thereof shall know it no more.

17. But the mercy of the **LORD** *is* from everlasting to everlasting upon them that fear him, and **his** righteousness unto children's children;

18. To such as keep **his** covenant, and to those that remember **his** commandments to do them.

19. The **LORD** hath prepared **his** throne in the heavens; and **his** kingdom ruleth over all.

20. BLESS THE **LORD**, ye **his** angels, that excel in strength, that do **his** commandments, hearkening unto the voice of **his** word.

21. BLESS YE THE LORD,
ALL YE HIS HOSTS:
YE MINISTERS OF HIS.
THAT DO HIS PLEASURE.

22. BLESS THE LORD,
ALL HIS WORKS
IN ALL PLACES OF HIS DOMINION;
BLESS THE LORD, O MY SOUL.

PSALM * CIV.

BLESS the LORD, O my soul, O LORD my GOD, thou art very great; thou art clothed with honour and majesty.

2. Who coverest **thyself** with light as with a garment: who stretchest out the heavens like a curtain:

3. Who layest the beams of **his** chambers in the waters: who maketh the clouds **his** chariot; who walketh upon the wings of the wind:

4. Who maketh **his** angels spirits; **his** ministers a flaming fire:

5. Who laid the foundations of the earth, that it should not be removed for ever.

6. **Thou** coveredst it with the deep as with a garment: the waters stood above the mountains.

7. At **thy** rebuke they fled; at the voice of **thy** thunder they hasted away.

8. They go up by the mountains; they go down by the valleys unto the place which **thou** hast founded for them.

9. **Thou** hast set a bound that they may not pass over; that they turn not again to cover the earth.

10. **He** sendeth the springs into the valleys, which run among the hills.

11. They give drink to every beast of the field: the wild asses quench their thirst.

12. By them shall the fowls of the heaven have their habitation, _which_ sing among the branches.

13. He watereth the hills from **his** chambers: the earth is satisfied with the fruit of **thy** works.

14. He causeth the grass to grow for the cattle, and herb for the service of man: that he may bring forth food out of the earth.

15. And wine _that_ maketh glad the heart of man, and oil to make _his_ face to shine, and bread _which_ strengtheneth man's heart.

16. The trees of the **LORD** are full _of sap_; the cedars of **Lebanon**, which he hath planted:

17. Where the birds make their nests: _as for_ the stork, the fir trees _are_ her house.

18. The high hills _are_ a refuge for the wild goats; _and_ the rocks for the conies.

19. He appointed the moon for seasons; the sun knoweth his going down.

20. Thou makest darkness, and it is night: wherein all the beasts of the forest do creep _forth._

21. The young lions roar after their prey, and seek their meat from **GOD.**

22. The sun ariseth, they gather themselves together, and lay them down in their dens.

23. Man goeth forth unto his work and to his labour until the evening.

24. O LORD, HOW MANIFOLD ARE THY WORKS! IN WISDOM HAST THOU MADE THEM ALL, THE EARTH IS FULL OF THY RICHES.

25. So is this great and wide sea, wherein are things creeping innumerable, both small and great beasts.

26. There go the ships: there is that leviathan, whom thou hast made to play therein.

27. These wait all upon thee; that thou mayest give them their meat in due season.

28. That thou givest them they gather; thou openest thine hand, they are filled with good.

29. Thou hidest thy face, they are troubled: thou takest away their breath, they die, and return to their dust.

30. Thou sendest forth thy spirit, they are created: and thou renewest the face of the earth.

31. The Glory of the Lord shall endure for ever: the Lord shall rejoice in his works.

32. He looketh on the earth, and it trembleth: he toucheth the hills, and they smoke.

33. I will sing unto the **LORD** as long as I live: I will sing praise to my **GOD** while I have my being.

34. **My** meditation of **him** shall be sweet: I will be glad in the **LORD**.

35. **Let** the sinners be consumed out of the earth, and let the wicked be no more.

Bless thou the Lord, O my soul.

Praise ye the Lord.

PSALM ✶ CV.

O GIVE thanks unto the LORD; call upon his name: make known his deeds among the people.

2. Sing unto him, sing psalms unto him: talk ye of all his wondrous works.

3. Glory ye in his holy name: let the heart of them rejoice that seek the LORD.

4. Seek the LORD, and his strength: seek his face evermore.

5. Remember his marvellous works that he hath done; his wonders, and the judgments of his mouth;

6. O ye seed of Abraham his servant, ye children of Jacob his chosen.

7. He is the LORD our GOD: his judgments are in all the earth.

8. He hath remembered his covenant for ever, the word which he commanded to a thousand generations.

9. Which covenant he made with Abraham, and his oath unto Isaac;

10. And confirmed the same unto Jacob for a law, and to Israel for an everlasting covenant:

11. Saying, Unto thee will I give the land of Canaan, the lot of your inheritance:

12. When they were but a few men in number; yea, very few, and strangers in it.

13. When they went from one nation to another, from one kingdom to another people:

14. He suffered no man to do them wrong: yea, He reproved kings for their sakes;

15. Saying, Touch not MINE anointed, and do my prophets no harm.

16. Moreover HE called for a famine upon the land: HE brake the whole staff of bread

17. He sent a man before them, even Joseph, who was sold for a servant:

18. Whose feet they hurt with fetters: he was laid in iron:

19. Until the time that his word came: the word of the LORD tried him.

20. The king sent and loosed him; even the ruler of the people and let him go free.

21. He made him lord of his house, and ruler of all his substance.

22. To bind his princes at his pleasure; and teach his senators wisdom

23. Israel also came into Egypt; and Jacob sojourned in the land of Ham.

24. And HE increased his people greatly; and made them stronger than their enemies.

25. He turned their heart to hate his people, to deal subtilly with his servants.

26. He sent Moses his servant; and Aaron whom HE had chosen.

27. They shewed his signs among them, and wonders in the land of Ham.

28. He sent darkness, and made it dark; and they rebelled not against his word.

He spake, and the locusts came,

29. He turned their waters into blood, and slew their fish.

30. Their land brought forth frogs in abundance, in the chambers of their kings.

31. He spake, and there came divers sorts of flies, and lice in all their coasts.

32. He gave them hail for rain, and flaming fire in their land.

33. He smote their vines also and their fig trees; and brake the trees of their coasts.

34. He spake, and the locusts came, and caterpillers, and that without number,

35. And did eat up all the herbs in their land, and devoured the fruit of their ground.

36. He smote also all the firstborn in their land, the chief of all their strength.

37. He brought them forth also with silver and gold: and *there was* not one feeble *person* among their tribes.

38. Egypt was glad when they departed: for the fear of them fell upon them.

39. He spread a cloud for a covering; and fire to give light in the night.

40. *The people* asked, and He brought quails, and satisfied them with the bread of heaven.

41. He opened the rock, and the waters gushed out; they ran in the dry places *like a river*.

42. For He remembered His holy promise, *and* Abraham His servant.

43. And He brought forth His people with joy, *and* His chosen with gladness:

44. And gave them the lands of the heathen: and they inherited the labour of the people:

45. That they might observe His statutes, and keep His laws.

Praise ye the LORD.

PSALM ✻ CVI.

PRAISE YE THE LORD.

O give thanks unto the LORD;
For HE is good:
for his mercy endureth for ever.

2. Who can utter the mighty acts of the LORD?
who can shew forth all his praise?

3. Blessed are they that keep judgment, and he that
doeth righteousness at all times.

4. Remember me, O LORD,
with the favour that
thou bearest unto thy
people: O visit me with
thy salvation;

5. That I may see the good of thy chosen, that
I may rejoice in the gladness of thy nation,
that I may glory with MINE inheritance.

6. We have sinned with our fathers, we have committed iniquity,
we have done wickedly.

7. Our fathers understood not thy wonders in Egypt; they
remembered not the multitude of thy mercies; but provoked
him at the sea, even at the Red sea.

8. Nevertheless he saved them for his name's sake, that he
might make his mighty power to be known.

9. He rebuked the Red sea also, and it was dried up: so
he led them through the depths, as through the wilderness.

10. And HE saved them
from the hand of him
that hated them, and redeemed
them from the hand of the enemy

11. And the waters covered
their enemies: there was not
one of them left.

12. Then believed they his words;
they sang his praise.

13. They soon forgat his works;
they waited not for his counsel:

14. But lusted exceedingly in the
wilderness, and tempted GOD
in the desert.

15. And HE gave them their request; but
sent leanness into their soul.

16. They envied Moses also in the camp, and Aaron
the saint of the LORD.

17. The earth opened and swallowed up Dathan, and covered
the company of Abiram.

18. And a fire was kindled in their company; the flame burned
up the wicked.

19. They made a calf in Horeb, and worshipped the molten
image.

20. Thus they changed their glory into the similitude of an ox
that eateth grass.

21. They forgat GOD their saviour, which had done great
things in Egypt:

22. Wondrous works in the land of Ham, and terrible
things by the Red sea.

23. Therefore HE said that HE would destroy them, had not Moses his chosen stood before HIM in the breach, to turn away his wrath, lest HE should destroy them.

24. Yea, they despised the pleasant land, they believed not his word:

25. But murmured in their tents, and hearkened not unto the voice of the LORD.

26. Therefore HE lifted up his hand against them, to over-throw them in the wilderness:

27. To overthrow their seed also among the nations, and to scatter them in the lands.

28. They joined themselves also unto Baalpeor, and ate the sacrifices of the dead.

29. Thus they provoked him to anger with their inventions: and the plague brake in upon them.

30. Then stood up Phinehas, and executed judgment: and so the plague was stayed.

31. And that was counted unto him for righteousness unto all generations for evermore.

32. They angered him also at the waters of strife, so that it went ill with Moses for their sakes:

33. Because they provoked his spirit, so that he spake unadvis-edly with his lips.

34. They did not destroy the nations, concerning whom the LORD commanded them:

35. But were mingled among the heathen, and learned their works.

36. And they served their idols: which were a snare unto them.

37. Yea, they sacrificed their sons and their daughters unto devils.

38. And shed innocent blood, even the blood of their sons and of their daughters, whom they sacrificed unto the idols of Canaan: and the land was polluted with blood.

39. Thus were they defiled with their own works, and went a whoring with their own inventions.

40. Therefore was the wrath of the **LORD** kindled against **his** people, insomuch that **he** abhorred **his** own inheritance.

41. And **he** gave them into the hand of the heathen; and they that hated them ruled over them.

42. Their enemies also oppressed them, and they were brought into subjection under their hand.

43. Many times did **he** deliver them, but they provoked **him** with their counsel, and were brought low for their iniquity.

44. Nevertheless **he** regarded their affliction, when **he** heard their cry:

45. And **he** remembered for them **his** covenant, and repented according to the multitude of **his** mercies.

46. **He** made them also to be pitied of all those that carried them captives.

47. Save us, O **LORD** our **GOD**, and gather us from among the heathen, to give thanks unto thy holy name, and to triumph in thy praise

48. Blessed be the **LORD GOD** of Israel from everlasting to everlasting:

and let all the people say, Amen.

Praise ye the LORD.

PSALM ✳ CVII.

O GIVE THANKS UNTO THE LORD, FOR *HE IS* GOOD: FOR HIS MERCY *ENDURETH* FOR EVER.

2. Let the redeemed of the LORD say so, whom HE hath redeemed from the hand of the enemy;

3. And gathered them out of the lands, from the east, and from the west, from the north, and from the south.

4. They wandered in the wilderness in a solitary way; they found no city to dwell in.

5. Hungry and thirsty, their soul fainted in them.

6. Then they cried unto the LORD in their trouble, *and* HE delivered them out of their distresses.

7. And HE led them forth by the right way, that they might go to a city of habitation.

8. Oh that *men* would praise the LORD *for* his goodness, and *for* his wonderful works to the children of men!

9. For HE satisfieth the longing soul. and filleth the hungry soul with goodness.

10. Such as sit in darkness and in the shadow of death, *being* bound in affliction and iron.

11. Because they rebelled against the words of GOD, and contemned the counsel of the most High:

12. Therefore **he** brought down their heart with labour; they fell down, and *there was* none to help.

13. Then they cried unto the **LORD** in their trouble, *and* **he** saved them out of their distresses.

14. **He** brought them out of darkness and the shadow of death, and brake their bands in sunder.

15. <u>Oh that *men* would praise the **LORD** *for* his goodness, and *for* his wonderful works to the children of men!</u>

16. For **he** hath broken the gates of brass, and cut the bars of iron in sunder.

17. Fools because of their transgression, and because of their iniquities, are afflicted.

18. Their soul abhorreth all manner of meat; and they draw near unto the gates of death.

19. Then they cry unto the **LORD** in their trouble, *and* **he** saveth them out of their distresses.

20. **He** sent **his** word, and healed them, and delivered <u>them</u> from their destructions.

21. <u>Oh that *men* would praise the **LORD** *for* his goodness, and *for* his wonderful works to the children of men!</u>

22. And let them sacrifice the sacrifices of thanksgiving, and declare **his** works with rejoicing.

23. They that go down to the sea in ships, that do business in great waters:

24. These see the works of the **LORD**, and **his** wonders in the deep.

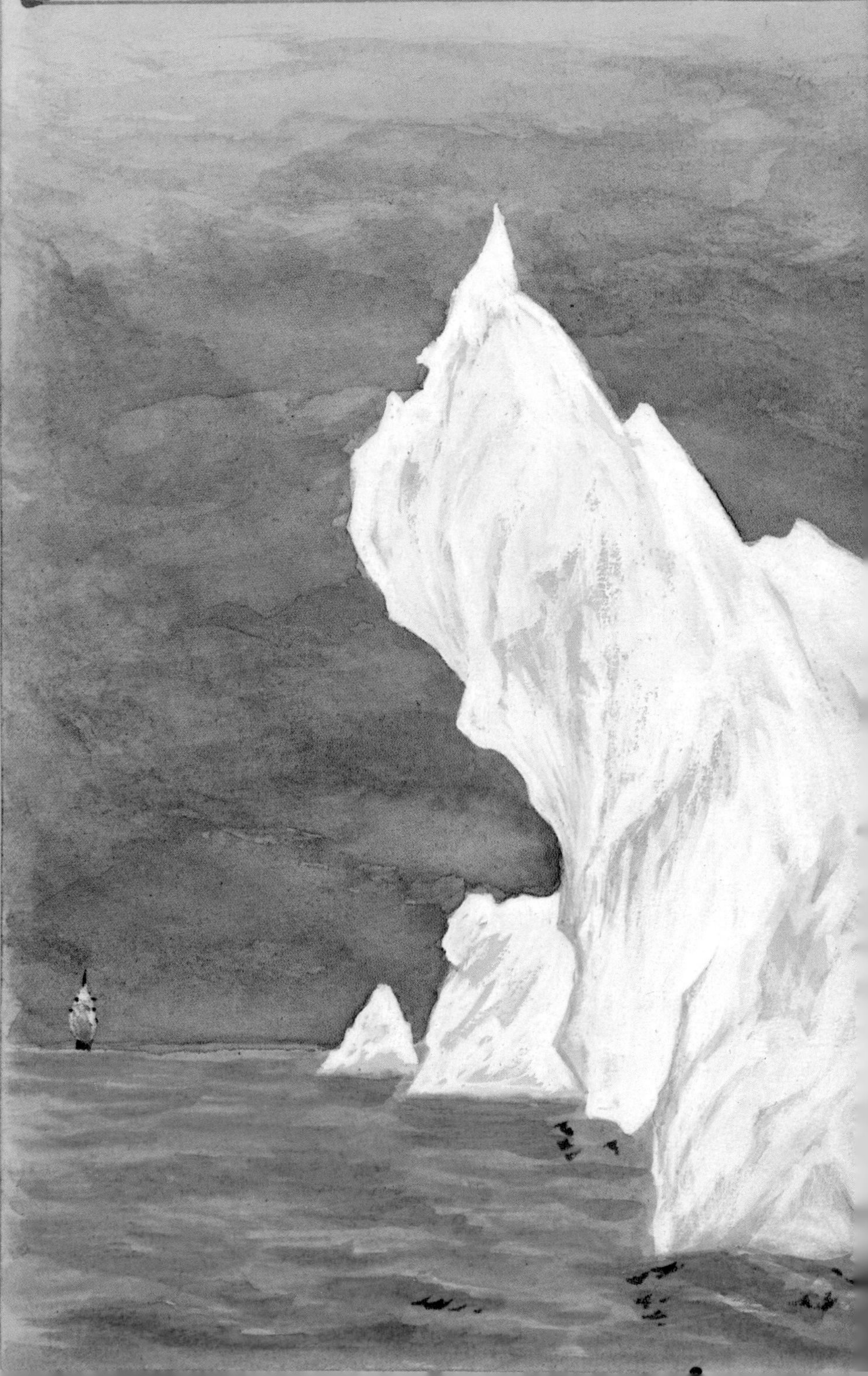

25. For **he** commandeth, and raiseth the stormy wind, which lifteth up the waves thereof.

26. They mount up to the heaven, they go down again to the depths: their soul is melted because of trouble.

27. They reel to and fro, and stagger like a drunken man, and are at their wit's end.

28. Then they cry unto the **LORD** in their trouble, and **he** bringeth them out of their distresses.

29. **He** maketh the storm a calm, so that the waves thereof are still.

30. Then are they glad because they be quiet; so **he** bringeth them unto their desired haven.

31. <u>Oh that *men* would praise the LORD *for* **his** goodness, and *for* **his** wonderful works to the children of men!</u>

32. Let them exalt **him** also in the congregation of the people, and praise **him** in the assembly of the elders.

33. **He** turneth rivers into a wilderness, and the watersprings into dry ground;

34. A fruitful land into barrenness, for the wickedness of them that dwell therein.

35. **He** turneth the wilderness into a standing water, and dry ground into watersprings.

36. And there **he** maketh the hungry to dwell, that they may prepare a city for habitation;

37. And sow the fields, and plant vineyards, which may yield fruits of increase.

38. **He** blesseth them also, so that they are multiplied greatly; and suffereth not their cattle to decrease.

39. **A**gain, they are minished and brought low through op-
-pression, affliction, and sorrow.

40. **He** poureth contempt upon princes, and causeth them
to wander in the wilderness, *where there is no way.*

41. **Y**et setteth **he** the poor on high from affliction, and
maketh *him* families like a flock.

42. **T**he righteous shall see *it*, and rejoice; and all iniquity
shall stop her mouth.

43. **W**hoso *is* wise, and will observe *these things*, even they
shall understand ____

<u>The lovingkindness of the LORD.</u>

PSALM ✦ CVIII.

A Song or Psalm of David.

O God. my heart is fixed; I will sing and give praise, even with my glory.

2. Awake, psaltery and harp: I myself will awake early.

3. I will praise **thee**, O **Lord**, among the people: and I will sing praises unto **thee** among the nations.

4. For **thy** mercy is great above the heavens; and **thy** truth reacheth unto the clouds.

5. Be thou exalted, O God, above the heavens; and **thy** glory above all the earth;

6. That thy beloved may be deliv-
-ered : save with thy right hand,
and answer me.

7. God hath spoken in his holiness;
I will rejoice, I will divide
Shechem, and mete out the val-
-ley of Succoth.

8. Gilead is Mine; Manasseh is
Mine; Ephraim also is the
strength of Mine head; Judah
is My lawgiver;

9. Moab is My washpot; over
Edom will I cast out My
shoe; over Philistia will I
triumph.

10. Who will bring me into the
strong city? who will lead
me into Edom?

11. Wilt not thou, O God, who
hast cast us off? and wilt
not thou, O God, go forth

with our hosts?

12. Give us help from trouble:
for vain is the help

of man.

13. Through

God

we shall

do valiantly:

for he it is that shall

tread down our

enemies.

PSALM ✳ CIX.

To the chief Musician,
A Psalm of David.

HOLD not thy peace,
O GOD of my praise;

2. For the mouth of the wicked and the
mouth of the deceitful are opened against me:
they have spoken against me with a lying tongue.

3. They compassed me about also with words of
hatred; and fought against me without
a cause.

4. For my love they are my adversaries: but I give
myself unto prayer.

5. And they have rewarded me evil for good, and hatred
for my love.

6. Set thou a wicked man over him: and let Satan
stand at his right hand.

7. When he shall be judged, let him be condemned:
and let his prayer become sin.

8. Let his days be few; and let another take his office.

9. Let his children be fatherless, and his wife a widow.

10. Let his children be continually vagabonds, and beg:
let them seek their bread also out of their desolate
places.

11. Let the extortioner catch all that he hath; and let the strangers spoil his labour.

12. Let there be none to extend mercy unto him: neither let there be any to favour his fatherless children.

13. Let his posterity be cut off; and in the generation following let their name be blotted out.

14. Let the iniquity of his fathers be remembered with the **LORD**; and let not the sin of his mother be blotted out.

15. Let them be before the **LORD** continually, that **he** may cut off the memory of them from the earth.

16. Because that he remembered not to shew mercy, but persecuted the poor and needy man, that he might even slay the broken in heart.

17. As he loved cursing, so let it come unto him: as he delighted not in blessing, so let it be far from him.

18. As he clothed himself with cursing like as with his garment, so let it come into his bowels like water, and like oil into his bones.

19. Let it be unto him as the garment which covereth him, and for a girdle wherewith he is girded continually.

20. Let this be the reward of mine adversaries from the **LORD**, and of them that speak evil against my soul.

21. But do **thou** for me, **O GOD** the **LORD**, for **thy** name's sake: because **thy** mercy is good, deliver **thou** me.

22. For I am poor and needy, and my heart is wounded within me.

23. I am gone like the shadow when it declineth: I am tossed up and down as the locust.

24. My knees are weak through fasting; and my flesh faileth of fatness.

25. I became also a reproach unto them: when they looked upon me they shaked their heads.

26. Help me, O LORD my GOD:
O save me according to THY mercy:

27. That they may know that this is THY hand; that THOU, LORD, hast done it.

28. Let them curse, but bless THOU: when they arise, let them be ashamed; but let THY servants rejoice.

29. Let mine adversaries be clothed with shame, and let them cover themselves with their own confusion, as with a mantle.

30. I will greatly praise the LORD with my mouth; yea, I will praise him among the multitude.

31. For HE shall stand at the right hand of the poor, to save him from those that condemn his soul.

PSALM ✶ CX.

A Psalm of David.

The LORD said unto my LORD,
Sit thou at my right hand,
until I make thine enemies
thy footstool.

2. The LORD shall send the rod of thy
strength out of Zion: rule thou in the
midst of thine enemies.

3. Thy people shall be willing in the day of thy
power, in the beauties of holiness
from the womb of the morning: thou hast
the dew of thy youth.

4. The LORD hath sworn, and will not repent,
thou art a priest for ever after the
order of Melchizedek.

5. The LORD at thy right hand shall strike through
kings in the day of his wrath.

6. He shall judge among the heathen, he shall fill
the places with the dead bodies; he shall
wound the heads over many countries.

7. He shall drink of the brook in the way : there-
-fore shall **he** lift up the head.

PSALM ✳ CXI.

PRAISE ye the **LORD**.
I will praise the **LORD** with
my whole heart, in the assembly
of the upright, and in the congregation

2. The works of the **LORD** are great, sough
out of all them that have pleasure therein.

3. His work is honourable and glorious: and
his righteousness endureth for ever.

4. He hath made **his** wonderful works to be remembere
the **LORD** is gracious and full of compassion.

5. He hath given meat unto them that fear **him** : he
will ever be mindfull of **his** covenant.

6. He hath shewed **his** people the power of **his**
works, that **he** may give them the heritage
of the heathen.

7. The works of his hands are verity and judgment; all his commandments are sure.

8. They stand fast for ever and ever, and are done in truth and uprightness.

9. He sent redemption unto his people: he hath commanded his covenant for ever: holy and reverend is his name.

10. The fear of the LORD is the beginning of wisdom: a good understanding have all they that do his commandments: his praise endureth for ever.

PSALM ✳ CXII.

PRAISE YE THE LORD.

Blessed is the man that feareth the LORD, that delighteth greatly in his commandments.

2. His seed shall be mighty upon earth : the gene-
-ration of the upright shall be blessed .

3. Wealth and riches *shall be* in his house : and his
righteousness endureth for ever .

4. Unto the upright there ariseth light in the dark-
-ness : *he is* gracious, and full of compassion,
and righteous .

5. A good man sheweth favour, and lendeth : he
will guide his affairs with discretion .

6. Surely he shall not be moved for ever : the righteous
shall be in everlasting remembrance .

7. He shall not be afraid of evil tidings : his heart is fixed,
<u>trusting in the LORD.</u>

8. His heart is established , he shall not be afraid, until
he see *his desire* upon his enemies.

9. He hath dispersed, he hath given to the poor ; his
righteousness endureth for ever ; his horn shall be
exalted with honour .

10 The wicked shall see *it*, and be grieved ; he shall
gnash with his teeth, and melt away : the desire
of the wicked shall perish .

PSALM * CXIII.

PRAISE ye the **LORD**.
   Praise, **O** ye servants of the **LORD**,
      praise the name of the **LORD**.

2. **B**lessed be the name of the **LORD** from this
   time forth and for evermore.

3. **F**rom the rising of the sun unto the going down of
   the same the **LORD'S** name *is* to be praised.

4. **T**he **LORD** *is* high above all nations, *and* **his**
   glory above the heavens.

5. **W**ho *is* like unto the **LORD** our **GOD**,
   who dwelleth on high.

6. **W**ho humbleth *himself* to behold *the things that*
   are in heaven, and in the earth!

7. **H**e raiseth up the poor out of the dust, *and* lifteth the
   needy out of the dunghill;

8. **T**hat **he** may set him with princes, *even* with the
   princes of his people.

9. **H**e maketh the barren woman to keep house, *and to be*
   a joyful mother of children.

Praise ye the **LORD**.

260.

PSALM ✳ CXIV.

WHEN Israel went out of Egypt, the house of **Jacob** from a peo--ple of strange language;

2. **Judah** was **his** sanctuary, and **Israel his** dominion.

3. The sea saw *it*, and fled; **Jordan** was driven back.

4. The mountains skipped like rams, *and* the little hills like lambs.

5. What *ailed* thee, **O** thou sea, that thou fleddest? thou **Jordan**, *that thou wast* driven back?

6. Ye mountains, *that* ye skipped like rams; *and ye* little hills, like lambs?

7. Tremble, thou earth, at the presence of the **LORD**, at the presence of the **GOD** of **Jacob**;

8. Which turned the rock *into* a standing water, the flint into a fountain of waters.

PSALM ✳ CXV.

NOT unto us,
    O LORD,
    not unto us,
    but unto thy name
    give glory,
    for thy mercy,
    and for thy truth's
        sake.

2. Wherefore should the
    heathen say,
    Where is now their
        GOD?

3. But our GOD is in
    the heavens: he
    hath done whatsoever he
    hath pleased.

4. Their idols are silver and
    gold, the work of men's hands.

5. They have mouths, but they speak not: eyes have they, but they see not:

6. They have ears, but they hear not: noses have they, but they smell not.

7. They have hands, but they handle not: feet have they, but they walk not: neither speak they through their throat.

8. They that make them are like unto them; so is every one that trusteth in them.

9. O Israel,

trust thou in the LORD:

he is their help and their shield.

10. O house of Aaron, trust in the LORD: he is their help and their shield.

11. Ye that fear the LORD, trust in the LORD: he is their help and their shield.

12. The LORD hath been mindful of us:

he will bless us:

he will bless the house of Israel; he will bless the house of Aaron.

13. He will bless them that fear the LORD, both small and great.

14. The LORD shall increase you
more and more,
you and your children.

15. Ye are blessed of the LORD which made heaven
and earth.

16. The heaven, even the heavens, are the LORD'S:
but the earth hath HE given to the children of men.

17. The dead praise not the LORD, neither any
that go down into silence.

18. But we will bless the LORD from this time forth
and for evermore.

Praise the LORD.

PSALM ✳ CXVI.

I LOVE the LORD. because HE hath
heard my voice and my supplications.

2. Because HE hath inclined his ear unto me, there-
-fore will I call upon him as long as I live.

3. The sorrows of death compassed me, and the pains of hell gat hold upon me: I found trouble and sorrow.

4. Then called I upon the name of the **LORD**; **O LORD**, I beseech **thee**, deliver my soul.

5. Gracious is the **LORD**, and righteous; yea, our **GOD** is merciful.

6. The **Lord** preserveth the simple: I was brought low, and **he** helped me.

7. Return unto thy rest, **O** my soul; for the **Lord** hath dealt bountifully with thee.

8. For **thou** hast delivered my soul from death, mine eyes from tears, *and* my feet from fall-ing.

9. I will walk before the **LORD** in the land of the living.

10. I believed, therefore have I spoken: I was greatly afflicted:

11. I said in my haste, All men are liars.

12. What shall I render unto the **LORD** for all **his** benefits toward me?

13. I will take the cup of salvation, and call upon the name of the **LORD**.

14. I will pay my vows unto the **LORD** now in the presence of all his people.

15. Precious in the sight of the **LORD** is the death of **his** saints.

16. O **LORD**, truly I am thy servant; I am thy servant, and the son of thine hand-maid: thou hast loosed my bonds.

17. I will offer to thee the sacrifice of thanksgiving, and will call upon the name of the **LORD**.

18. I will pay my vows unto the **LORD** now in the presence of all **his** people.

19. In the courts of the **LORD'S** house, in the midst of thee. O Jerusalem.

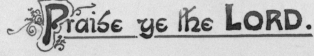 Praise ye the **LORD**.

PSALM CXVII.

O Praise the **LORD**, all ye nations: praise him all ye people.

2. For **his** merciful kindness is great toward us: and the truth of the **LORD** endureth for ever. Praise ye the **LORD**.

PSALM ✳ CXVIII.

O Give thanks unto the LORD,
for HE is good:
because his mercy
endureth for ever.

2. Let Israel now say, that
his mercy endureth for ever.

3. Let the house of Aaron now say, that
his mercy endureth for ever.

4. Let them now that fear the LORD say, that
his mercy endureth for ever.

5. I called upon the LORD in distress: the LORD
answered me, and set me in a large place.

6. The LORD is on my side; I will not fear:
what can man do unto me?

7. The LORD taketh my part with them that help me:
therefore shall I see my desire upon them that
hate me.

8. It is better to trust in the LORD than to put con-
-fidence in man.

9. It is better to trust in the **LORD** than to put con--fidence in princes.

10. All nations compassed me about: but in the name of the **LORD** will I destroy them.

11. They compassed me about; yea, they compassed me about: but in the name of the **LORD** I will destroy them.

12. They compassed me about like bees; they are quenched as the fire of thorns: for in the name of the **LORD** I will destroy them.

13. Thou hast thrust sore at me that I might fall: bu

the LORD helped me.

14. The **LORD** is my strength and song, and is become my salvation.

15. The voice of rejoicing and salvation is in the tabernacles of the righteous:

the right hand of the **LORD** doeth valiantly.

16. The right hand of the **LORD** is exalted: the right hand of the **LORD** doeth valiantly.

17. I shall not die, but live, and declare the works of the **LORD**:

18. The **LORD** hath chastened me sore: but **HE** hath not given me over unto death.

19. Open to me the gates of righteousness: I will go into them, and I will praise the **LORD**:

20. This gate of the **LORD**, into which the right- -eous shall enter.

21. I will praise **thee**: for **thou** hast heard me, and art become my salvation.

22. The stone *which* the builders refused is become the head *stone* of the corner.

23. This is the **LORD'S** doing; it *is* marvellous in our eyes.

24. This *is* the day *which* the **LORD** hath made; we will rejoice and be glad in it.

25. Save now, I beseech thee, O **LORD**: O **LORD**, I beseech thee, send now prosperity.

26. Blessed *be* he that cometh in the name of the LORD: we have blessed you out of the house of the LORD.

27. GOD *is* the LORD, which hath shew- -ed us light: bind the sacrifice with cords, *even* unto the horns of the altar.

28. Thou art my GOD, and I will praise Thee: *thou art* my GOD, I will exalt Thee.

29. O give thanks unto the LORD, for *he is* good: for his mercy endureth for ever.

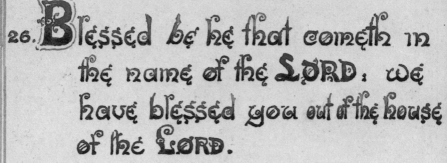

PSALM ✻ CXIX.

ALEPH.

Beati immaculati.

BLESSED are the undefiled in the way, who walk in the law of the LORD.

2. Blessed are they that keep **his** testimonies, and that seek **him** with the whole heart.

3. They also do no iniquity: they walk in **his** ways.

4. **Thou** hast commanded us to keep **thy** precepts diligently.

5. O that my ways were directed to keep **thy** statutes.

6. Then shall I not be ashamed, when I have respect unto all thy commandments.

7. I will praise **thee** with uprightness of heart, when I shall have learned **thy** righteous judgments.

8. I will keep **thy** statutes: O forsake me not utterly.

BETH. In quo corriget?

9. Wherewithal shall a young man cleanse his way? by taking heed thereto according to **thy** word.

10. With my whole heart have I sought **thee** : O let me not wander from **thy** commandments.

11. **Thy** word have I hid in mine heart, that I might not sin against **thee**.

12. **B**lessed art **thou, O LORD** : teach me **thy** statutes.

13. With my lips have I declared all the judgments of **thy** mouth.

14. I have rejoiced in the way of **thy** testimonies. as much as in all riches.

15. I will meditate in **thy** precepts, and have respect unto **thy** ways.

16. I will delight myself in **thy** statutes : I will not forget **thy** word.

GIMEL . Retribue servo tuo.

17. **D**eal bountifully with **thy** servant, that I may live, and keep **thy** word.

18. **O**pen **thou** mine eyes, that I may behold wondrous things out of **thy** law.

19. I am a stranger in the earth : hide not **thy** commandments from me.

20. **M**y soul breaketh for the longing that it hath unto **thy** judgments at all times.

21. **Thou** hast rebuked the proud that are cursed. which do err from **thy** commandments.

22. **R**emove from me reproach and contempt; for I have kept **thy** testimonies.

23. Princes also did sit and speak against me : but **Thy** servant did meditate in **thy** statutes.

24. **Thy** testimonies also are my delight and my counsellors.

DALETH. Adhæsit pavimento.

25. **M**y soul cleaveth unto the dust : quicken **thou** me according to **thy** word.

26. **I** have declared my ways, and **thou** heard-est me : **teach me thy statutes**.

27. **M**ake me to understand the way of **thy** precepts : so shall **I** talk of **thy** wondrous works.

28. **M**y soul melteth for heaviness : strengthen **thou** me according unto **thy** word.

29. **R**emove from me the way of lying : and grant me **thy** law graciously.

30. **I** have chosen the way of truth : **thy** judgments have **I** laid before me.

31. **I** have stuck unto **thy** testimonies : **O LORD**, put me not to shame.

32. **I** will run the way of **thy** commandments, when **thou** shall enlarge my heart.

HE. Legem pone.

33. **T**each me, **O LORD**, the way of **thy** statutes ; and **I** shall keep it unto the end.

34. **G**ive me understanding, and **I** shall keep **thy** law ; yea, **I** shall observe it with my whole heart.

35. Make me to go in the path of **thy** command-
-ments; for therein do I delight.

36. Incline my heart unto **thy** testimonies,
and not to covetousness.

37. Turn away mine eyes from beholding vanity;
and quicken thou me in **thy** way.

38 Stablish **thy** word unto **thy** servant, who
is devoted to **thy** fear.

39. Turn away my reproach which I fear: for
thy judgments are good.

40. Behold, I have longed after **thy** precepts:
quicken me in **thy** righteousness.

VAU. Et veniat super me.

41. Let **thy** mercies come also unto me, O LORD,
even **thy** salvation, according to **thy** word.

42. So shall I have wherewith to answer him that
reproacheth me: for I trust in **thy** word.

43. And take not the word of truth utterly out of
my mouth; for I have hoped in **thy** judgments

44. So shall I keep **thy** law continually for ever
and ever.

45. And I will walk at liberty: for I seek **thy**
precepts.

46. I will speak of **thy** testimonies also before
kings, and will not be ashamed.

47. And I will delight myself in **thy** command-
-ments, which I have loved.

48. **My** hands also will I lift up unto **thy**
commandments, which I have loved; and
I will meditate in **thy** statutes.

ZAIN. Memor esto servi tui.

49. Remember the word unto **thy** servant, upon
which **thou** hast caused me to hope.

50. This is my comfort in my affliction: for **thy**
word hath quickened me.

51. The proud have had me greatly in derision:
yet have I not declined from **thy** law.

52. I remembered **thy** judgments of old, **O LORD**:
and have comforted myself.

53. Horror hath taken   hold upon me because
of the wicked
that forsake **thy**
law.

54. **Thy** statutes have
been my songs in
the house
of my pilgrimage.

55. I have remembered **thy** name, **O LORD**, in the night, and have kept **thy** law.

56. This I had, because I kept **thy** precepts.

CHETH. <u>Portio mea, Domine.</u>

57. **Thou** art my portion, **O LORD**, I have said that I would keep **thy** words.

58. I intreated **thy** favour with my whole heart: be merciful unto me according to **thy** word.

59. I thought on my ways, and turned my feet unto **thy** testimonies.

60. I made haste, and delayed not to keep **thy** commandments.

61. **The** bands of the wicked have robbed me: but I have not forgotten **thy** law.

62. **At** midnight I will rise to give thanks unto **thee** because of **thy** righteous judgments.

63. I am a companion of all them that fear **thee**. and of them that keep **thy** precepts.

64. **The** earth, **O LORD**, is full of **thy** mercy: teach me **thy** statutes.

TETH. <u>Bonitatem fecisti.</u>

65. **Thou** hast dealt well with **thy** servant. **O LORD**, according unto **thy** word.

66. Teach me good judgment and knowledge: for I have believed **thy** commandments.

67. Before I was afflicted I went astray: but now have I kept **thy** word.

68. Thou art good, and doest good; teach me **thy** statutes.

69. The proud have forged a lie against me: but I will keep **thy** precepts with my whole heart.

70. Their heart is as fat as grease; but I delight in **thy** law.

71. It is good for me that I have been afflicted: that I might learn **thy** statutes.

72. The law of **thy** mouth is better unto me than thousands of gold and silver.

JOD. Manus tuæ fecerunt me

73. **Thy** hands have made me and fashioned me: give me understanding, that I may learn **thy** commandments.

74. They that fear **thee** will be glad when they see me; because I have hoped in **thy** word.

75. I know, **O LORD**, that **thy** judgments are right, and that **thou** in faithfulness hast afflicted me.

76. Let, I pray **thee**, **thy** merciful kindness be for my comfort, according to **thy** word unto **thy** servant.

77. Let **thy** tender mercies come unto me, that I may live: for **thy** law is my delight.

78. Let the proud be ashamed: for they dealt perversely with me without a cause: but I will meditate in **thy** precepts.

79. Let those that fear **thee** turn unto me, and those that have known **thy** testimonies.

80. Let my heart be sound in **thy** statutes; that I be not ashamed.

CAPH. <u>Defecit anima mea.</u>

81. My soul fainteth for **thy** salvation: but I hope in **thy** word.

82. Mine eyes fail for **thy** word, saying when will **thou** comfort me?

83. For I am become like a bottle in the smoke; yet do I not forget **thy** statutes.

84. How many are the days of **thy** servant? when will **thou** execute judgment on them that per-
-secute me?

85. The proud have digged pits for me, which are not after **thy** law.

86. All **thy** commandments are faithful: they per-
-secute me wrongfully; help **thou** me.

87. They had almost consumed me upon earth; but I forsook not **thy** precepts.

88. Quicken me after **thy** lovingkindness; so shall I keep the testimony of **thy** mouth.

LAMED. In æternum, Domine.

89. For ever, O LORD, **thy** word is settled in heaven.

90. Thy faithfulness is unto all generations: thou hast estab--lished the earth, and it abideth.

91. They continue this day according to thine ordinances: for all are thy servants.

92. Unless thy law had been my delights I should then have perished in mine affliction.

93. I will never forget thy precepts: for with them thou hast quickened me.

94. I am thine, save me; for I have sought thy precepts.

95. The wicked have waited for me to destroy me: but I will consider thy testimonies.

96. I have seen an end of all perfection: but thy commandment is exceeding broad.

MEM. Quomodo dilexi!

97. O how love I thy law! it is my meditation all the day.

98. Thou through thy commandments hast made me wiser than mine enemies: for they are ever with me.

99. I have more understanding than all my teachers for thy testimonies are my meditation.

100. I understand
more than the ancients,
because I keep **thy** precepts.

101. I have refrained my feet from every evil way,
that I might keep **thy** word.

102. I have not departed from **thy** judgments: for
thou hast taught me.

103. **How** sweet are **thy** words unto my taste! yea,
sweeter than honey to my mouth!

104. **Through thy** precepts I get understanding:
therefore I hate every false way.

NUN. Lucerna pedibus meis.

105. Thy word is a lamp unto my
feet, and a light unto my
path.

106. I have sworn, and I will perform it, that I will keep thy righteous judgments.

107. I am afflicted very much: quicken me, O **LORD**, according unto **thy** word.

108. Accept, I beseech **Thee**, the freewill offerings of my mouth, **O LORD**, and teach me **thy** judgments.

109. My soul is continually in my hand: yet do I not forget **thy** law.

110. The wicked have laid a snare for me: yet I erred not from **thy** precepts.

111. **Thy** testimonies have I taken as an heritage for ever: for they are the rejoicing of my heart.

112. I have inclined mine heart to perform **thy** statutes alway, even unto the end.

SAMECH. Iniquos odio habui.

113. I hate vain thoughts: but **thy** law do I love.

114. Thou art my hiding place and my shield: I hope in **thy** word.

115. Depart from me, ye evildoers: for I will keep the commandments of my **GOD**.

116. Uphold me according unto **thy** word, that I may live: and let me not be ashamed of my hope.

117. Hold thou me up, and I shall be safe: and I
will have respect unto thy statutes continually.

118. Thou hast trodden down all them that err from
thy statutes: for their deceit is falsehood.

119. Thou puttest away all the wicked of the earth like
dross: therefore I love thy testimonies.

120. My flesh trembleth for fear of thee; and I am
afraid of thy judgments.

AIN. Feci judicium.

121. I have done judgment and justice: leave me not
to mine oppressors.

122. Be surety for thy servant for good: let not the
proud oppress me.

123. Mine eyes fail for thy salvation, and for the
word of thy righteousness.

124. Deal with thy servant according unto thy
mercy, and teach me thy statutes.

125. I am thy servant; give me understanding, that
I may know thy testimonies.

126. It is time for thee, LORD, to work: for they
have made void thy law.

127. Therefore I love thy commandments above gold,
yea, above fine gold.

128. Therefore I esteem all thy precepts concerning
all things to be right; and I hate every false way.

PE. Mirabilia.

129. Thy testimonies are wonderful: therefore doth my soul keep them.

130. The entrance of **thy** words giveth light; it giveth understanding unto the simple.

131. I opened my mouth, and panted: for I longed for **thy** commandments.

132. Look **thou** upon me, and be merciful unto me, as **thou** usest to do unto those that love **thy** name.

133. Order my steps in **thy** word: and let not any iniquity have dominion over me.

134. Deliver me from the oppression of man: so will I keep **thy** precepts.

135. Make **thy** face to shine upon **thy** servant; and and teach me **thy** statutes.

136. Rivers of waters run down mine eyes, because they keep not **thy** law.

TZADDI. Justus es, Domine.

137. Righteous art **thou**, O LORD, and up=-right are **thy** judgments.

138. Thy testimonies that **thou** hast command-ed are righteous and very faithful.

139. My zeal hath consumed me, because mine enemies have forgotten **thy** words.

140. Thy word is very pure : therefore thy servant loveth it.

141. I am small and despised : yet do not I forget thy precepts.

142. Thy righteousness
is an everlasting
righteousness.
and thy law is the truth.

143. Trouble and anguish have taken hold on me : yet thy commandments are my delights.

144. The righteousness of thy testimonies is ever--lasting :

give me understanding,
and I shall live.

KOPH. Clamavi in toto corde meo.

145. I cried with my whole heart ; hear me, O LORD: I will keep thy statutes.

146. I cried unto THEE ; save me, and I shall keep thy testimonies.

147. I prevented the dawning of the morning, and cried : I hoped in thy word.

148. Mine eyes prevent the night watches, that I might meditate in **thy** word.

149. Hear my voice according unto **thy** lovingkind- -ness: O LORD, quicken me according to **thy** judgment.

150. They draw nigh that follow after mischief: they are far from **thy** law.

151. <u>Thou art near</u>, **O LORD**; and all **thy** commandments are truth.

152. Concerning **thy** testimonies, I have known of old that **thou** hast founded them for ever.

RESH. <u>Vide humilitatem.</u>

153. Consider mine affliction, and deliver me: for I do not forget **thy** law.

154. Plead my cause, and deliver me: quicken me accord- -ing to **thy** word.

155. Salvation is far from the wicked: for they seek not **thy** statutes.

156. Great are **thy** tender mercies, **O LORD**: quick- -en me according to **thy** judgments.

157. Many are my persecuters and mine enemies; yet do I not decline from **thy** testimonies.

158. I beheld the transgressors, and was grieved; because they kept not **thy** word.

159. Consider how I love thy precepts: quicken me, O LORD, according to thy loving-kindness.

160. Thy word is true from the beginning: and every one of thy righteous judgments endureth for ever.

SCHIN. Principes persecuti sunt.

161. Princes have persecuted me without a cause: but my heart standeth in awe of thy word.

162. I rejoice at thy word, as one that findeth great spoil.

163. I hate and abhor lying: but thy law do I love.

164. Seven times a day do I praise thee because of thy righteous judgments.

165. Great peace have they which love thy law: and nothing shall offend them.

166. LORD, I hoped for thy salvation, and done thy commandments.

167. My soul hath kept thy testimonies; and I love them exceedingly.

168. I have kept thy precepts and thy testimonies: for all my ways are before thee.

TAU. Appropinquet deprecatio.

169. Let my cry come near before thee, O LORD: give me understanding according to thy word.

170. Let my supplication come before **Thee**: deliver me according to **Thy** word.

171. My lips shall utter praise, when **Thou** hast taught me **Thy** statutes.

172. My tongue shall speak of **Thy** word : for all **Thy** commandments are righteous.

173. Let **Thine** hand help me ; for **I** have chosen **Thy** precepts.

174. **I** have longed for **Thy** salvation, **O LORD**; and **Thy** law is my delight.

175. Let my soul live, and it shall praise **Thee** ; and let **Thy** judgments help me.

176. **I** have gone astray like a lost sheep; seek **Thy** servant; for **I** do not forget **Thy** commandments.

PSALM ✸ CXX.

A Song of degrees.

IN my distress **I** cried unto the **LORD**, and **he** heard me.

2. Deliver my soul, **O LORD**, from lying lips, and from a deceitful tongue.

3. What shall be given unto thee? or what shall be done unto thee, thou false tongue?

4. Sharp arrows of the mighty, with coals of juniper.

5. Woe is me, that I sojourn in Mesech, that I dwell in the tents of Kedar!

6. My soul hath long dwelt with him that hateth peace.

7. I am for peace: but when I speak, they are for war.

PSALM ✳ CXXI.

A Song of degrees.

I Will lift up mine eyes unto the hills, from whence cometh my help.

2. My help cometh from the LORD, which made heaven and earth.

3. He will not suffer thy foot to be moved: he that keepeth thee will not slumber.

4. Behold, he that keepeth Israel shall neither slumber nor sleep.

5. The Lord is thy keeper: the Lord is thy shade upon thy right hand.

6. The sun shall not smite thee by day, nor the moon by night.

7. The Lord shall preserve thee from all evil: He shall preserve thy soul.

8. The Lord shall preserve thy going out and thy coming in from this time forth, and even for evermore.

PSALM ✳ CXXII.

A Song of degrees of David.

I WAS glad when they said unto me, Let us go into the house of the LORD.

2. Our feet shall stand within thy gates, O Jerusalem.

3. Jerusalem is builded as a city that is compact together:

4. Whither the tribes go up, the tribes of the **Lord**, unto the testimony of **Israel**, to give thanks unto the name of the **Lord**.

5. For there are set thrones of judgment, the thrones of the house of **David**.

6. Pray for the peace of **Jerusalem**: they shall prosper that love thee.

7. Peace be within thy walls, and prosperity with-in thy palaces.

8. For my brethren and companions sakes, I will now say, Peace be within thee.

9. Because of the house of the **Lord** our **God** I will seek thy good.

PSALM ✳ CXXIII.

A Song of degrees.

UNTO Thee lift I up mine eyes, O Thou that dwellest in the heavens.

2. Behold, as the eyes of servants look unto the hand of their masters, and as the eyes of a maiden unto the hand of her mistress; so our eyes wait upon the **Lord** our **God**, until that **He** have mercy upon us.

3. Have mercy upon us, O Lord,
    have mercy upon us:
    for we are exceedingly filled with contempt.

4. Our soul is exceedingly filled with the scorning
    of those that are at ease, and with the contempt
    of the proud.

PSALM ✶ CXXIV.

A Song of degrees of David.

IF it had not been the Lord who was on our
    side, now may Israel say;

2. If it had not been the Lord who was on our
    side, when men rose up against us:

3. Then they had swallowed us up quick, when
    their wrath was kindled against us:

4. Then the waters had overwhelmed us, the
    stream had gone over our soul:

5. Then the proud waters had gone over our soul.

6. Blessed be the Lord, who hath not
    given us as a prey to their teeth.

7. Our soul is escaped as a bird out of the snare of
    the fowlers: the snare is broken, and we are escaped.

8. Our help is in the name of the **Lord**, who made heaven and earth.

PSALM ✺ CXXV.

A Song of degrees.

They that trust in the **LORD** shall be as mount **Zion**, which cannot be removed, but abideth for ever.

2. As the mountains are round about
   Jerusalem,
   so the **LORD** is round about **his** people
   from henceforth even for ever.

3. For the rod of the wicked shall not rest upon
   the lot of the righteous; lest the righteous
   put forth their hands unto iniquity.

4. Do good, **O LORD**, unto those that be good, and
   to them that are upright in their hearts.

5. As for such as turn aside unto their crooked ways.
   the **LORD** shall lead them forth with the workers
   of iniquity: but peace shall be upon **Israel**.

PSALM ✳ CXXVI.

A Song of degrees.

When the Lord turned
again the captivity of
Zion, we were like them
that dream.

2. Then was our mouth filled with
laughter, and our tongue with
singing: then said they among
the heathen, The Lord hath done
great things for them.

3. The Lord hath done great things
for us; whereof we are glad.

4. Turn again our captivity, O Lord,
as the streams in the South.

5. They that sow in tears
shall reap in joy.

3. He that goeth forth and
weepeth, bearing precious
seed, shall doubtless come
again with rejoicing,
bringing his sheaves with him.

PSALM ✳ CXXVII.

A Song of degrees for Solomon.

Except the Lord build the
house, they labour in vain that build
it: except the Lord keep the city, the
watchman waketh but in vain.

2. It is vain for you to rise up early, to sit up late,
to eat the bread of sorrows; for so he giveth
his beloved sleep.

3. Lo, children are an heritage of the Lord:
and the fruit of the womb is his reward.

4. As arrows are in the hand of a mighty man;
so are children of the youth.

5. Happy is the man that hath his quiver full of them: they shall not be ashamed, but they shall speak with the enemies in the gate.

PSALM CXXVIII.
A Song of degrees.

Blessed is every one that feareth the Lord; that walketh in his ways.

2. For thou shalt eat the labour of thine hands: happy shalt thou be, and it shall be well with thee

3. Thy wife shall be as a fruitful vine by the sides of thine house: thy children like olive plants round about thy table.

4. Behold, that thus shall the man be blessed that feareth the Lord.

5. The Lord shall bless thee out of Zion: and thou shalt see the good of Jerusalem all the days of thy life.

6. Yea, thou shalt see thy children's children, and peace upon Israel.

PSALM ✷ CXXIX.

A Song of degrees.

Many a time have they afflicted me from my youth, may **Israel** now say:

2. Many a time have they afflicted me from my youth: yet they have not prevailed against me.

3. The plowers plowed upon my back: they made long their furrows.

4. **The Lord is righteous**: HE hath cut asunder the cords of the wicked.

5. Let them all be confounded and turned back that hate **Zion**.

6. Let them be as the grass upon the housetops, which withereth afore it groweth up.

7. Wherewith the mower filleth not his hand; nor he that bindeth sheaves his bosom.

8. Neither do they which go by say, The blessing of the **Lord** be upon you: we bless you in the name of the **Lord**.

Psalm ☩ CXXX.

De profundis.

Out of the depths have I cried unto thee, O Lord.

2. Lord, hear my voice: let thine ears be attentive to the voice of my supplications.

3. If thou, Lord shouldest mark iniquities, O Lord, who shall stand?

4. But there is forgiveness with thee, that thou mayest be feared.

5. I wait for the Lord, my soul doth wait, and in his word do I hope.

6. My soul waiteth for the Lord more than they that watch for the morning: I say, more than they that watch for the morning.

7. Let Israel hope in the Lord: for with the Lord there is mercy, and with him is plenteous redemption.

8. And HE shall redeem Israel from all his iniquities.

PSALM ✳ CXXXI.

Domine, non est.

LORD, my heart is not haughty,
  nor mine eyes lofty: neither
    do I exercise myself in great matters,
    or in things too high for me.

2. Surely I have behaved and quieted myself,
  as a child that is weaned of his mother:
    my soul is even as a weaned child.

3. Let Israel hope in the Lord from
  henceforth and for ever.

PSALM ✳ CXXXII.

Memento Domine.

LORD, remember David, and all his
  afflictions:

2. How he sware unto the Lord, and vowed
  unto the mighty GOD of Jacob;

3. Surely I will not come into the tabernacle of
  my house, nor go up into my bed;

4. I will not give sleep to mine eyes, or slumber to
  mine eyelids.

5. Until I find out a place for the Lord, an habitation for the mighty GOD of Jacob.

6. Lo, we heard of it at Ephratah: we we found it in the fields of the wood.

7. We will go unto his tabernacles: we will worship at his footstool.

8. Arise, O Lord, into thy rest; thou, and the ark of thy strength.

9. Let thy priests be clothed with righteousness; and let thy saints shout for joy.

10. For thy servant David's sake turn not away the face of thine anointed.

11. The Lord hath sworn in truth unto David; he will not turn from it; Of the fruit of thy body will I set upon thy throne.

12. If thy children will keep my covenant and my testimony that I shall teach them, their children shall also sit upon thy throne for evermore.

13. For the Lord hath chosen Zion; he hath desired it for his habitation.

14. This is my rest for ever; here will I dwell; for I have desired it.

15. I will abundantly bless her provision: I will satisfy her poor with bread.

16. I will also clothe her priests with salvation: and her saints shall shout aloud for joy.

17. There will I make the horn of David to bud:
I have ordained a lamp for MINE anointed.
18. His enemies will I clothe with shame: but
upon himself shall his crown flourish.

PSALM ✳ CXXXIII.

Ecce, quam bonum!

Behold, how good and how pleasant
it is for brethren to dwell together in unity.
2. It is like the precious ointment upon the head,
that ran down upon the beard, even Aaron's
beard: that went down to the skirts of his
garments;
3. As the dew of Hermon,
and as the dew that descended upon the
mountains of Zion:
for there the Lord commanded
the blessing,
even life for evermore.

PSALM CXXXIV.

Ecce nunc.

Behold, bless ye the Lord,
all ye servants of the Lord,
which by night stand in the house of
the Lord.

2. Lift up your hands in the Sanctuary,
and bless the Lord.

3. The Lord that made heaven
and earth bless thee
out of Zion.

PSALM CXXXV.

Laudate Nomen.

Praise ye the Lord.
Praise ye the name of the Lord;
praise him,
O ye servants of the Lord.

2. Ye that stand in the house of the **Lord**, in the courts of the house of our **GOD**,

3. Praise the **Lord**; for the **Lord** is good: sing praises unto **his** name;
for it is pleasant.

4. For the **Lord** hath chosen **Jacob** unto himself, and **Israel** for **his** peculiar treasure.

5. For **I** know the **Lord** is great, and that our **Lord** is above all gods.

6. Whatsoever the **Lord** pleased, that did **he** in heaven, and in earth, in the seas, and all deep places.

7. **He** causeth the vapours to ascend from the ends of the earth; **he** maketh lightnings for the rain; he bringeth the wind out of **his** treasuries.

8. **Who** smote the first-born of **Egypt**, both of man and beast.

9. **Who** sent tokens and wonders into the midst of thee, **O Egypt**, upon **Pharaoh**, and upon all his servants.

10. **Who** smote great nations, and slew mighty kings:

11. **Sihon** king of the **Amorites**, and **Og** king of **Bashan**, and all the kingdoms of **Canaan:**

12. **And** gave their land for an heritage, an heritage unto **Israel his** people.

13. **Thy name, O Lord,** <u>endureth</u> **for ever;** and **thy memorial, O Lord,** throughout all generations.

14. **For** the **Lord** will judge **his** people, and **he** will repent **himself** concerning **his** servants.

15. **The** idols of the heathen <u>are</u> silver and gold, the work of men's hands.

16. **They** have mouths, but they speak not; eyes have they, but they see not;

17. **They** have ears, but they hear not; neither is there <u>any</u> breath in their mouths.

18. **They** that make them <u>are</u> like unto them: so is every one that trusteth in them.

19. **Bless** the **Lord, O** house of **Israel:** **Bless** the **Lord, O** house of **Aaron.**

20. Bless the Lord, O house of Levi: ye that fear the Lord, bless the Lord.

21. Blessed be the Lord out of Zion, which dwelleth at Jerusalem.

Praise ye the Lord.

PSALM CXXXVI.

Confitemini.

O GIVE thanks unto the Lord; for HE is good:
for his mercy endureth for ever.

2. O give thanks unto the GOD of gods:
for his mercy endureth for ever.

3. O give thanks to the Lord of lords:
for his mercy endureth for ever.

4. To him who alone doeth great wonders:
for his mercy endureth for ever.

5. To him that by wisdom made the heavens:
for his mercy endureth for ever.

6. To him that stretched out the earth above
the waters:
for his mercy endureth for ever.

7. To him that made great lights:
for his mercy endureth for ever.

8. The sun to rule by day:
for his mercy endureth for ever.

9. The moon and stars to rule by night:
for his mercy endureth for ever.

10. To him that smote Egypt in their
firstborn:
for his mercy endureth for ever.

11. And brought out Israel from among them:
for his mercy endureth for ever.

12. With a strong hand, and with a stretched
out arm:
for his mercy endureth for ever.

13. To him which divided the Red sea
into parts:
for his mercy endureth for ever.

14. And made Israel to pass through the
midst of it:
for his mercy endureth for ever.

15. But overthrew **Pharaoh** and his host in the **Red** sea :
      for **his** mercy endureth for ever.

16. **To him** which led **his** people through the wilderness :
      for **his** mercy endureth for ever.

17. **To him** which smote great kings :
      for **his** mercy endureth for ever.

18. **And** slew famous kings :
      for **his** mercy endureth for ever.

19. **Sihon** king of the **Amorites** :
      for **his** mercy endureth for ever.

20. **And Og** the king of **Bashan** :
      for **his** mercy endureth for ever.

21. **And** gave their land for an heritage :
      for **his** mercy endureth for ever.

22. **Even** an heritage unto **Israel his** servant :
      for **his** mercy endureth for ever.

23. **Who** remembered us in our low estate :
      for **his** mercy endureth for ever.

24. **And** hath redeemed us from our enemies :
      for **his** mercy endureth for ever.

25. **Who** giveth food to all flesh :
      for **his** mercy endureth for ever.

26. **O** give thanks unto
      the God of heaven :
      for **his** mercy endureth for ever.

PSALM ✳ CXXXVII.

Super flumina.

By the rivers of Babylon,
there we sat down,
yea, we wept,
when we remembered Zion.

2. We hanged our harps
  -upon the willows
  in the midst thereof.

3. For there they
  that carried us away captive
  required of us a song;
  and they that wasted us
  required of us mirth,
  saying,
  Sing us one of the songs of Zion.

4. How shall we sing the Lord's song
  in a strange land?

5. If I forget thee,
  O Jerusalem,
  let my right hand forget her cunning.

6. If I do not remember thee.
  let my tongue cleave to the roof of my mouth;
  if I prefer not Jerusalem
  above my chief joy.

7. Remember, O Lord,
the children of Edom
in the day of Jerusalem;
who said, Rase it, rase it,
even to the foundation thereof.

8. O daughter of Babylon,
who art to be destroyed;
happy shall he be,
that rewardeth thee as thou hast served us.

9. Happy shall he be,
that taketh and dasheth
thy little ones against the stones.

PSALM CXXXVIII.

A Psalm of David.

Confitebor tibi.

I will praise Thee with my whole heart:
before the gods will I sing praise
unto Thee.

2. I will worship toward Thy holy temple, and
praise Thy name for Thy lovingkindness
and for Thy truth: for Thou hast magni-
-fied Thy word above all Thy name.

3. In the day when I cried thou answeredst me, and strengthenedst me with strength in my soul.

4. All the kings of the earth shall praise Thee, O Lord, when they hear the words of thy mouth.

Daisies, thou flowers of lowly birth,
   Embroiderers of the carpet earth,
      That gem the velvet sod;
Open to Spring's refreshing air,
   In sweetest, smiling bloom declare,
      Your Maker, and my God.

5. Yea, they shall sing in the ways of the
Lord : for
great is the glory of the Lord.

6. Though the Lord be high, yet hath
HE respect unto the lowly : but the proud
HE knoweth afar off.

7. Though I walk in the midst of trouble, thou
wilt revive me : thou shalt stretch forth
thine hand against the wrath of mine
enemies, and thy right hand shall save me.

8. The Lord will perfect that which concerneth
me :
thy mercy, O Lord, endureth
for ever :
forsake not the works of thine own hands.

PSALM ✳ CXXXIX.

To the chief Musician, A Psalm of David.

Domine probasti.

O Lord, thou hast searched me,
and known me.

2. Thou knowest my downsitting and
mine uprising, thou understandest my
thought afar off.

3. **Thou** compassest my path
and my lying down,
and art acquainted
with all my ways.

4. **F**or there is not
a word in my tongue,
but, lo, **O Lord**,
Thou knowest it altogether.

5. **Thou** hast beset me
behind and before,
and laid **thine** hand
upon me.

6. **S**uch knowledge is
too wonderful for me;
it is high,
I cannot attain unto it.

7. **W**hither shall **I** go
from **thy spirit?**
or whither shall **I** flee
from **thy** presence?

8. **I**f **I** ascend up into heaven,
thou art there:
if **I** make my bed in hell,
behold, **thou** art there.

9. **I**f **I** take
the wings of the morning,
and dwell
in the uttermost parts of the sea;

10. Even there
shall thy hand lead me,
and thy right hand shall hold me.

11. If I say, Surely
the darkness shall cover me;
even the night shall be light about me.

12. Yea, the darkness
hideth not from thee;
but the night
shineth as the day:
the darkness and the light
are both alike to thee.

13. For thou hast possessed my reins:
thou hast covered me
in my mother's womb.

14. I will praise thee;
for I am fearfully and wonderfully made:
marvellous are thy works;
and that my soul knoweth right well.

15. My substance was not hid from thee,
when I was made in secret,
and curiously wrought
in the lowest parts of the earth.

16. Thine eyes did see my substance,
yet being imperfect; and in thy book all my
members were written, which in continuance
were fashioned, when as yet there was none
of them.

17. How precious also
are thy thoughts
unto me, O God!
how great is
the sum of them!

18. If I should count them,
they are more in number
than the sand:
when I awake,
I am still with thee.

19. Surely thou wilt slay the wicked,
O God:
depart from me therefore,
ye bloody men.

20. For they speak against thee wickedly,
and thine enemies
take thy name in vain.

21. Do not I hate them,
O Lord,
that hate thee?
and am I not grieved
with those
that rise up against thee?

22. I hate them with perfect hatred:
I count them mine enemies.

23. Search me, O God,
and know my heart:
try me,
and know my thoughts:

24. And see if there be any wicked way in me
and lead me
in the way everlasting.

PSALM ✳ CXL.

To the chief Musician, A Psalm of David.

Eripe me Domine.

Deliver me, O Lord,
from the evil man: preserve me from the
violent man;

2. Which imagine mischiefs in their heart;
continually are they gathered together
for war.

3. They have sharp-
-ened their tongues
like a serpent;
adders' poison
is under their
lips.
Selah.

4. Keep
me,
O
Lord,
from
the hands
of the wicked;
preserve me from
the violent man;
who have purposed to
overthrow my goings.

5. The proud have hid a snare for me, and cords; they have spread a net by the wayside; they have set gins for me. Selah.

6. I said unto the **Lord**, **Thou art my God**: hear the voice of my supplication, **O Lord**.

7. **O God the Lord**, the strength of my salvation, **thou** hast covered my head in the day of battle.

8. Grant not, **O Lord**, the desires of the wicked: further not his wicked device; lest they exalt themselves. Selah.

9. As for the head of those that compass me about, let the mischief of their own lips cover them.

10. Let burning coals fall upon them: let them be cast into the fire; into deep pits, that they rise not up again.

11. Let not an evil speaker be established in the earth: evil shall hunt the violent man to overthrow him.

12. I know that ____ the Lord will maintain the cause of the afflicted, and the right of the poor.

13. Surely the righteous shall give thanks unto thy name: the upright shall dwell in thy presence.

PSALM CXLI.

A Psalm of David.

Domine clamavi.

Lord, I cry unto thee:
make haste unto me;
give ear unto my voice,
when I cry unto thee.

2. Let my prayer be set forth
before thee as an incense;
and the lifting up of my hands
as the evening sacrifice.

3. Set a watch, O Lord.
before my mouth;
keep the door of my lips.

4. Incline not my heart to any evil
thing, to practise wicked works
with men that work iniquity: and
let me not eat of their dainties.

5.

Let
the righteous
smite me;
it shall be a kindness:
and let him reprove me;
it shall be an excellent oil,
which shall not break my
head: for yet my
prayer also shall
be in their
calamities.

6. When their judges
are overthrown in stony
places, they shall hear my
words; for they are sweet.

4

7. Our bones are scattered at the grave's mouth, as when one cutteth and cleaveth wood upon the earth.

8. But mine eyes are unto thee, O God the Lord: in thee is my trust; leave not my soul destitute.

9. Keep me from the snares which they have laid for me, and the gins of the workers of iniquity.

10. Let the wicked fall into their own nets, whilst that I withal escape.

PSALM CXLII.

Maschil of David;
A Prayer when he was in the cave.
Voce mea ad Dominum.

I cried unto the Lord with my voice; with my voice unto the Lord did I make my supplication.

2. I poured out my complaint before **him**; I shewed before **him** my trouble.

3. When my spirit was overwhelmed within me, then **thou** knewest my path. In the way wherein I walked have they privily laid a snare for me.

4. I looked on my right hand, and behold, but there was no man that would know me: refuge failed me; no man cared for my soul.

5. I cried unto **thee**, **O Lord**: I said,

Thou art my refuge and my portion in the land of the living.

6. Attend unto my cry; for **I** am brought very low: deliver me from my perse-cutors; for they are stronger than **I**.

7. **B**ring my soul out of prison, that **I** may praise **thy** name: the righteous shall compass me about; for **thou** shalt deal bountifully with me.

5

PSALM CXLIII.

A Psalm of David.

Domine exaudi.

Hear my prayer, O Lord, give ear to my supplications: in thy faithfulness answer me, and in thy righteousness.

2. And enter not into judgment with thy servant: for in thy sight shall no man living be justified.

3. For the enemy hath persecuted my soul; he hath smitten my life down to the ground; he hath made me to dwell in darkness, as those that have been long dead.

4. Therefore is my spirit overwhelmed within me; my heart within me is desolate.

5. I remember the days of old; I meditate on all thy works; I muse on the work of thy hands.

6. I stretch forth my hands unto thee: my soul thirsteth after thee, as a thirsty land. Selah.

7. Hear me speedily, O Lord: my spirit faileth: hide not thy face from me, lest I be like unto them that go down into the pit.

8. Cause me to hear **thy** lovingkindness in the morning; for in **thee** do I trust: cause me to know the way wherein I should walk; for I lift up my soul unto **thee**.

9. Deliver me, **O Lord**, from mine enemies: I flee unto **thee** to hide me.

10. Teach me to do **thy** will; for **thou art my God**; **thy spirit is good**; lead me into the land of uprightness.

11. Quicken me, **O Lord**, for **thy** name's sake: for **thy** righteousness' sake bring my soul out of trouble.

12. And of **thy** mercy cut off mine enemies, and destroy all them that afflict my soul: for I am **thy** servant.

6

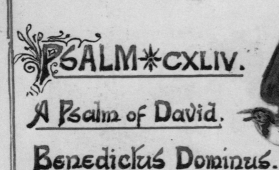

PSALM ✻ CXLIV.

A Psalm of David.

Benedictus Dominus.

Blessed be the Lord my
Strength, which teacheth my hands
to war, *and my fingers to fight*:

2. My goodness, and my fortress;
my high tower, and my deliv-
-erer; my Shield, and *he*
in whom I trust;

who subdueth
my people under me.

3. **Lord**, what is man,
that **thou** takest know-
-ledge of him! or the
son of man, that
thou makest account
of him!

4. **Man** is like to vanity:
his days are as a shadow
that passeth away.

5. **Bow thy heavens,
O Lord**, and come
down: touch the mountains,
and they shall smoke.

6. **Cast** forth lightning, and
scatter them: shoot out
thine arrows, and
destroy them.

7. **Send thine hand**
from above;

rid me, and deliver me out of great waters, from the hand of strange chil- -dren;

8. Whose mouth speaketh vanity, and their right hand is a right hand of falsehood.

9. I will sing a new song unto thee, O GOD: upon a psaltery and an in- -strument of ten strings will I sing praises unto thee.

10. It is he that giveth salvation unto kings: who delivereth David his servant from the hurtful sword.

11. Rid me, and deliver me from the hand of strange children, whose mouth speaketh vanity, and their right hand is a right hand of falsehood:

12. That our sons *may be* as plants grown up in their youth; *that* our daughters *may be* as corner stones, polished *after* the similitude of a palace:

13. That our garners *may be* full, affording all manner of store; *that* our sheep may bring forth thousands and ten thousands in our streets:

14. That our oxen *may be* strong to labour; *that there be* no breaking in, nor go- -ing out; *that there be* no complaining in our streets.

15. Happy *is that* people, *that is* in such a case: *yea.*

Happy *is that* people, whose God is the Lord.

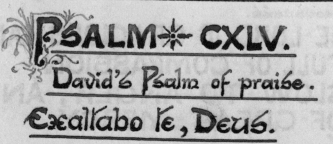

Psalm ⁕ CXLV.

David's Psalm of praise.

Exaltabo te, Deus.

I WILL extol thee, my GOD, O KING; and I will bless thy name for ever and ever.

2. Every day will I bless thee; and I will praise thy name for ever and ever.

3. Great is the LORD, and greatly to be praised; and his great=ness is unsearchable.

4. One generation shall praise thy works to ano=ther, and shall declare thy mighty acts.

5. I will speak of the glorious honour of thy majesty, and of thy wondrous works.

6. And men ~~shall~~ shall speak of the might of thy ter=rible acts: and I will declare thy greatness.

7. They shall abundantly utter the memory of thy great goodness, and shall sing of thy right=eousness.

8. THE LORD IS GRACIOUS, AND FULL OF COMPASSION; SLOW TO ANGER, AND OF GREAT MERCY.

9. THE LORD IS GOOD TO ALL: AND HIS TENDER MERCIES ARE OVER ALL HIS WORKS.

10. ALL THY WORKS SHALL PRAISE THEE, O LORD; AND THY SAINTS SHALL BLESS THEE.

11. They shall speak of the glory of thy kingdom, and talk of thy power;

12. To make known to the sons of men his mighty acts, and the glorious majesty of his kingdom.

13. Thy kingdom is an everlasting kingdom, and thy dominion endureth throughout all generations.

14. The Lord upholdeth all that fall, and raiseth up all *those that be bowed down*.

15. The eyes of all wait upon THEE; and thou givest them their meat in due season.

16. Thou openest thine hand, and satis-fiest the desire of every living thing.

17. The LORD is righteous in all his ways, and holy in all his works.

18. THE LORD IS NIGH UNTO ALL THEM THAT CALL UPON HIM, TO ALL THAT CALL UPON HIM IN TRUTH.

19. He will fulfil the desire of them that fear him: he also will hear their cry, and will save them.

20. The LORD preserveth all them that love him:
but all the wicked will HE destroy.
21. My mouth shall speak the praise of the LORD:
and let all flesh bless his holy name
for ever and ever.

PSALM CXLVI.

Lauda, anima mea.

PRAISE ye the LORD.

Praise the LORD, O my soul.
2. While I live will I praise the LORD: I will
sing praises unto my GOD while I have
any being.
3. Put not your trust in princes, nor in the son
of man, in whom *there is* no help.
4. His breath goeth forth, he return-eth to his earth;
in that very day his thoughts
perish.
5. Happy is he that
hath the
GOD of
Jacob for
his help,

whose hope *is* in the Lord
his GOD:

6. Which made heaven, and earth,
the sea, and all that therein *is:*
which keepeth truth for ever:

7. Which executeth judgment for the oppress-
-ed: which giveth food to the hungry.
The Lord looseth the prisoners:

8. The Lord openeth *the eyes* of the blind:
the Lord raiseth them that are bowed
down: the Lord loveth the righteous:

9. The Lord preserveth the strangers;
he relieveth the fatherless and widow:
but the way of the wicked he turneth
upside down.

10. The Lord shall reign for ever,
even thy God, O Zion,
unto all generations.
Praise ye the Lord.

PSALM CXLVII.

Laudate Dominum.

Praise ye the Lord: for *it is* good to sing praises unto our **GOD**; for *it is* pleasant; and praise is comely.

2. The **Lord** doth build up **Jerusalem**: he gathereth together the outcasts of **Israel**.

3. **He** healeth the broken in heart, and bindeth up their wounds.

4. **He** telleth the number of the stars; he calleth them all by *their* names.

5. **Great** *is* our **Lord**, and of great power: his understanding *is* infinite.

6. The **Lord** lifteth up the meek: he casteth the wicked down to the ground.

7. **Sing** unto the **Lord** with thanksgiving; sing praise upon the harp unto our **GOD**:

8. **Who** covereth the heaven with clouds, who prepareth rain for the earth, who maketh grass to grow upon the mountains.

9. **He** giveth to the beast his food, and to the young ravens which cry.

10. He delighteth not in the strength of the horse; he taketh not pleasure in the legs of a man.

11. The Lord taketh pleasure in them that fear him, in those that hope in his mercy.

12. Praise the Lord, O Jerusalem;
praise thy GOD, O Zion.

13. For HE hath strengthened the bars of thy
gates; HE hath blessed thy children
within thee.

14. HE maketh peace in thy borders, and fill-
-eth thee with the finest of the wheat.

15. HE sendeth forth HIS commandment
upon earth: HIS word runneth very
swiftly.

16. HE giveth snow like wool: HE scattereth
the hoar frost like ashes.

17. HE casteth forth HIS ice like morsels:
who can stand before HIS cold?

18. HE sendeth out HIS word, and melteth
them: HE causeth HIS wind to blow,
and the waters flow.

19. HE sheweth HIS word unto Jacob,
HIS statutes and HIS judgments
unto Israel.

20. HE hath not dealt so with any nation:
and as for HIS judgments, they have
not known them.
Praise ye the Lord.

PSALM ✦ CXLVIII.

Laudate Dominum.

Praise ye the Lord.

Praise ye the Lord from the heavens: praise him in the heights.

2. Praise ye him, all his angels: praise ye him, all his hosts.

3. Praise ye him, sun and moon: praise him all ye stars of light.

4. Praise him, ye heavens of heavens, and ye waters that be above the heavens.

5. Let them praise the name of the **Lord**: for **he** commanded, and they were crea-
-ted.

6. **He** hath also stablished them for ever and ever: **he** hath made a decree which shall not pass.

7. Praise the **Lord** from the earth, ye dragons, and all deeps:

8. Fire, and hail; snow and vapours; stormy wind fulfilling **his** word:

9. Mountains, and all hills; fruitful trees, and all cedars:

10. Beasts, and all cattle; creeping things, and flying fowl:

11. Kings of the earth, and all people; princes, and all judges of the earth:

12. Both young men, and maidens; old men, and children:

13. Let them praise the name of the **Lord**: for **his** name alone is excellent: **his** glory is above the earth and heaven.

14. **He** also exalteth the horn of **his** people, the praise of all **his** saints; even of the children of **Israel**, a people near unto **him**. Praise ye the **Lord**.

Psalm CXLIX.

Cantate Domino.

Praise ye the LORD.

Sing unto the Lord a new song, and his praise in the congregation of saints.

2. Let Israel rejoice in him that made him: let the children of Zion be joyful in their King.

3. Let them praise his name in the dance: let them sing praises unto him with the timbrel and harp.

4. For the LORD taketh pleasure in his people: he will beautify the meek with salvation.

5. Let the saints be joyful in glory: let them sing aloud upon their beds.

6. Let the high praises of GOD be in their mouth, and a two-edged sword in their hand;

7. To execute vengeance upon the heathen, and punishments upon the people.

8. To bind their kings with chains, and their nobles with fetters of iron;

9. To execute upon them the judgment written: this honour have all his saints.

Psalm ✳ CL.

Laudate Dominum.

Praise ye the LORD.
Praise GOD in HIS sanctuary. praise HIM in the firmament of HIS power.

2. Praise HIM for HIS mighty acts: praise HIM according to HIS excellent greatness.

3. Praise HIM with the sound of the trumpet: praise HIM with the psaltery and harp.

4. Praise HIM with the timbrel and dance: Praise HIM with stringed instruments and organs.

5. Praise HIM upon the loud cymbals. praise HIM upon the high sounding cymbals.

6. Let every thing that hath breath praise the LORD.

Praise ye the LORD.

THE END.